Boston
and the American Revolution

Boston National Historical Park
Massachusetts

Produced by the
Division of Publications
National Park Service

U.S. Department of the Interior
Washington, D.C.

National Park Handbooks are published to support
the National Park Service's management programs
and to promote understanding and enjoyment of
the more than 370 National Park System sites that
are important examples of our nation's natural and
cultural heritage. Each handbook is intended to be
informative reading and a useful guide before, during, and after a park visit. They are sold at parks
and can be purchased by mail from the Superintendent of Documents, U.S. Government Printing Office, Washington, DC 20402-9325. This is handbook
146.

Library of Congress Cataloging-in-Publication Data
Boston and the American Revolution/Boston National Historical Park, Boston, Massachusetts; produced by the Division of Publications, National Park Service, U.S. Department
of the Interior, Washington, D.C.
p.   cm.—(National park handbook series; 146)
Includes bibliographical references and index.
ISBN 0-912627-65-4
1. Boston (Mass.)—History—Revolution, 1775-1783.
2. Freedom Trail (Boston, Mass.) I. Boston National Historical Park (Boston, Mass.) II. United States. National Park Service. Division of Publications. III. Series: Handbook (United
States, National Park Service, Division of Publications); 146.
F73.B755 1998
974.4'6102—dc21   98-4483 CIP

Domestic ware, like this "No Stamp Act" teapot, often carried propaganda messages prior to the Revolution. The background image is part of a panoramic view of Boston in 1769.

A Revolutionary Era

Foreword

To travel back to Revolutionary Boston—to understand the people, events, and ideals of more than two centuries ago—is a great leap for us today. But the sites along the Freedom Trail do speak eloquently of that time—a time when Boston was not a sprawling metropolis but a moderate-sized seaport. Still, we need to look beyond what lies before our eyes, because 18th-century Boston was very different from the city we see today. Engineers had not yet reconfigured the landscape, and the town was confined to a peninsula, connected with the rest of the province of Massachusetts only by a narrow strip of land, called "the Neck" at Roxbury. In 1765, roughly 15,000 people lived on that peninsula in nearly 1,700 houses, mostly wooden structures crowded along the crooked, narrow streets and alleyways.

Walking the streets of 1765, visitors saw a busy and varied scene. There was the densely settled North End, Boston's first real neighborhood, where sailors and maritime artisans clustered. In the middle of town were shops, dwellings, and prominent public buildings—most notably the Old State House (then known as the Towne House) where the governing bodies of the Massachusetts Bay Colony and the town convened. In front of the Old State House, State Street (then called King Street) ran east to Long Wharf, which reached out a third of a mile into the harbor to welcome ships of all sizes. Boston also boasted impressive Georgian mansions. Especially in the southern wards and west near the Common, the town's well-to-do merchants and government officials resided in brick houses with spacious private gardens. Everywhere church spires pierced the skyline, reflecting the town's founding in religious fervor, while stores, workshops, wharves, and warehouses marked the area as a bustling commercial center.

Boston had an excellent harbor. In a very real sense, the town faced out toward the Atlantic. The ocean was the great highway of the 18th century. It did not isolate Bostonians but connected them to others. By mid-century, Boston ships sailed to the rich fishing banks off Nova Scotia, to the West Indian sugar islands, to continental colonies along the coast to Georgia, to southern Europe, and to various port cities of Great Britain.

With all of these parts of the Atlantic world, Bostonians had important economic dealings. With England, however, they felt a deeper tie as well, for Massachusetts was a colony of Great Britain. Britain was the source of political liberty, the mother country, and, as many called it, home. In 1750, few Bostonians imagined looking for liberty by separating from Britain. They did not imagine independence.

Within two decades of 1750, however, Bostonians were resisting the policies of the British government. Quickly, their resistance turned to revolution. In the span of a generation, they came to see themselves and their society in a new way. Today the sites of Boston National Historical Park include the scenes of critical events in the story: resolutions in defense of colonial rights made in town meetings at Faneuil Hall; the Boston Massacre in front of the Old State House; mass assemblies at Old South Meeting House that preceded the Boston Tea Party; the battle at Bunker Hill and the occupation of Dorchester Heights. What brought Americans to these sites on these occasions? The answer lies partly in the acts of British authorities, whose policies aroused a fervent opposition. It lies, too, in the townspeople's most basic beliefs and cherished ideals, most especially a notion of "liberty" that was precious not only to 18th-century Bostonians but ultimately to other Americans as well.

These pages explore Bostonians' idea of liberty. We have often seen that idea through the eyes and actions of the city's most prominent men. Yet liberty was also the vision of 18th-century shipwrights and shoemakers, barrelmakers and goodwives, tavern-keepers, shopkeepers, and sailors. The full story of Boston's revolution includes the beliefs and political practices that an assorted, often anonymous group known as "the people" brought with them to the conflict with Britain. Popular ideas of liberty both supported and challenged the city's leading men. As Boston's ordinary people found new ways to participate in public life, they made the era a truly revolutionary one. Inspired by the Revolution's ideals, later generations carried the logic of liberty still further to argue for the abolition of slavery, women's rights, and the right of working people to organize. For many people around the world the principles that the Revolution embodied have served as models of self-government and personal freedom.

Boston in the Empire

John Rowe *(inset left)* was in many ways typical of Boston merchants. Born in England to a family of means, he emigrated to Boston in the mid-1730s, at about age 21. After buying a warehouse along the Long Wharf, shown here in a 1764 watercolor, he set up to import fabrics, salt, and other goods. Later, he owned his own dock, "Rowe's Wharf." He profited within the empire, as he gained lucrative contracts for supplying the British Navy and as the lax enforcement of trade laws allowed him to smuggle Dutch tea. His fortune grew. He built a fine house in the fashionable South End of town, with vegetable gardens and a pasture for sheep. He joined social clubs, became a prominent Freemason, and worshipped at Trinity Church. He spent many evenings with fellow merchants at the British Coffee House at the head of the Long Wharf, discussing ways to improve "the state of trade." He was a prudent and respectable man. But in the 1760s and 1770s, John Rowe would become a reluctant revolutionary. Hard times and new Parliamentary policies set merchants like Rowe on a collision course with English authorities.

Bostonians of the mid-18th century were thankful to be part of the British Empire. More than a century earlier, the town's founders had consciously decided to leave some aspects of English life behind. But the Puritan settlers of the 1630s did not intend to separate from England. Instead, they sought to create in the Massachusetts Bay Colony a shining example of a godly commonwealth, "a City upon a Hill." Their society would be a "New" England, and its example would show the Old World the way to righteousness. For a short time it seemed that their experiment would succeed. In freezing winters and summer heat, settlers carved out farms, built religious meeting-houses, and established institutions of government for the province and the towns. They pursued their callings—their daily work as farmers and goodwives, shoemakers and smiths, traders, clergymen, and magistrates—with piety and diligence.

New Englanders watched expectantly as the society they had left was plunged into turmoil. When English Puritans took power during the Civil War of the 1640s, it seemed that Old England might follow the lead of Massachusetts Bay. But the Puritan commonwealth collapsed, and the decidedly un-Puritan Charles II was restored to the throne in 1660. After that, inhabitants of Massachusetts could no longer see themselves as leading England to righteousness. Where once they had imagined themselves on the cutting edge of history, the restoration of the Stuarts meant they were in danger of becoming a backwater.

Growing numbers of churches and new denominations demonstrated that spiritual ideals remained compelling to many townspeople. In the 18th century, however, Boston was tied to England less by religion than by economic trade, a shared history, and shared political culture.

A century earlier, by 1650, the mercantile nations of Europe had turned the whole Atlantic basin into a single trading area. Late in the 17th century, English

George III ascended the British throne in 1760 and lost no time in heeding his mother's words, "George, be a King!" After ousting popular Prime Minister William Pitt and winning control over Parliament by passing out royal gifts and favors to the right people, he sought ways to tighten his control over the American colonies. In doing so, he helped to foster a revolution. This 1771 portrait by Johann Zoffany portrays George III as commander in chief of the British Army.

traders and government officials turned their attention to establishing a commercial empire. From the European point of view, the most lucrative of the New World colonies were the sugar islands of the Caribbean. In England, sugar—once an expensive luxury consumed only by the aristocracy—became a staple in the diets of many. Caribbean planters scrambled to maximize production and imported enslaved Africans for back-breaking labor in the sugar cane fields. The southern continental colonies, too, had discovered a lucrative cash crop. As early as the 1620s, a tobacco boom led planters in Virginia to base their society, in the words of King James I, "on smoak." In the 18th century, traders in Pennsylvania, New York, New Jersey, Maryland, and Delaware began drawing wheat from the countryside to ship to Old World markets. Middle colony trade expanded rapidly around this essential foodstuff. The region would always enjoy a good market for its crops, quipped the essayist Thomas Paine, "while eating is the custom of Europe."

In the midst of this good fortune, New England merchants were at a disadvantage. Farmers in the region raised livestock and garden crops, cut timber and planted corn, but no single product found a substantial market abroad. To pay for English cloth, hardware, and other manufactures, New England merchants learned to diversify. They combined a variety of products—timber, potash, beef, whale oil, shingles—in a single cargo. They filled a niche in the carrying trade, using the region's timber supply to build ships and the region's labor supply to sail them. New England ships carried Carolina rice to England and Pennsylvania wheat to Europe. Some also plied the route to southern Europe, trading provisions for wine from Spain, Portugal, and the Canary Islands. Finally, the region's traders found a nearly insatiable market for timber, cattle, and dried fish in the Caribbean, where West Indies planters devoted all their land to sugar alone. New England ships supplied staples, then returned home with molasses for New England distillers to make into rum. Rum sales provided credit to purchase goods from England. From this commerce, a good many Boston merchants gradually built up fortunes. At the same time, they created complex business and cultural ties that located Boston firmly in the empire.

By the mid-18th century, trade had given a distinctive shape to Boston society. Only a handful of the port's population of 15,000 were merchants—about 250 in the early 1760s, if we reserve the term for men like John Rowe, who owned enough capital to engage directly in overseas trade and sell mostly at wholesale. Many more made a living as retailers. Their number fluctuated from good times to bad, and they ranged from large-scale shopkeepers to marginal dealers, men and women, who sold goods on the side as they kept a tavern, took in boarders, or managed an artisan shop. Artisans—called mechanics or tradesmen—included carpenters, caulkers, ropemakers, sailmakers, coopers, and others who directly served the maritime economy. Still others in the luxury trades lived off merchants' prosperity: fine silversmiths, like Paul Revere, peruke (wig) makers, tailors and dressmakers, coachmakers, carpenters and masons, fine furniture makers—all thrived as mercantile fortunes grew. One step removed were tradesmen who served more middle class or "middling" town consumers, but the livelihood of butchers, bakers, and shoemakers ultimately relied on the state of trade as well. Finally, within the laboring classes, there were fishermen who sailed for mackerel and cod; sailors—called "jack tars"—who manned the merchant fleet; workers at the wharves, stevedores and common laborers who did the hauling of cargo and materials so essential to the port city. There were laborers in the construction trades and in the ropewalks, as well as women who eked by as laundresses, servants, and seamstresses.

Although they shared a stake in seaborne commerce, town dwellers did not benefit equally from trade. Contemporaries took for granted the existence of inequality. Many loosely divided the town into the "better sort," the "middling sort," and the lower or "meaner sort." Successful professionals—doctors, lawyers, or clergymen educated at Harvard—and government officials appointed from England joined wealthy merchants in the first category. The most prosperous of these men and their families were marked off from their social inferiors by fashionable imported clothing, refined manners, and an opulent style of life.

Many more townspeople inhabited the middling world of shopkeepers and artisans. Tradesmen alone

Overseas trade routes were as critical to 18th-century Bostonians as highways are to Americans today. Ships brought port dwellers essential imports such as manufactured goods, sugar, molasses, and fruit. They also provided means to export such desired items as fish, naval timbers, whale oil, and rum. The extent to which Boston merchants were involved in all aspects of the transatlantic and coastal trade in the pre-Revolutionary War era is reflected on the large map. Wealthy Bostonians poured their capital into the highly lucrative but risky overseas trade. Less wealthy merchants satisfied themselves with coastal trade from Newfoundland to the West Indies. Boston ships carried naval stores, such as lumber and pine pitch for caulking ships, to Britain and Europe; sugar, molasses, and fruit from the West Indies to New England and Europe; and fish, lumber, livestock, and grain from New England to the West Indies. They called at western African ports to bring slaves and gold to the West Indies and North America. Although relatively few slaves were brought to Boston, the slave trade and the slave economy figured prominently in Boston's Atlantic trade network.

Before the Revolution, Boston merchants were deeply involved in many aspects of transatlantic and coastal commerce. Boston (map, right) *depended on a complex web of trade routes that bound the port's livelihood to the international marketplace. The newspaper advertisement announces the availability of a typical imported item.*

The Salem-based 45-ton, two-masted schooner Baltick *was the type of vessel favored by New Englanders for fishing and the coastal trade. Built in Newbury, Massachusetts, in 1763,* Baltick *was active in the transatlantic trade as well.*

BROWN SUGARS

Juſt Imported, and to be ſold cheap for Caſh only, by

BENJAMIN ANDREWS, jun.

Oppoſite the Swing-Bridge ;
Who ſells alſo,

New-England Rum, Philadelphia ſuperfine and common Flour, Ship Bread, race and ground ginger, copperas, allum, redwood, logwood, brimſtone, Liſbon ſalt, jar oyl, felt hats, wool cards, ſheetings, crown ſoap, Iron hollow ware, tar, oakham, and a parcel of ſmall well aſſorted lignum vitæ.

Boston's wealthiest shipowners regularly bought and sold slaves, which provided capital to purchase English manufactured goods. More significantly, much of Boston's trade depended directly on the slavery system of the southern colonies and the Caribbean. For example, Boston's ships carried fish to feed plantation slave laborers and slave-produced molasses supplied the New England rum industry. Wealthy traders profited most from the lucrative maritime commerce. Most Bostonians, however, derived some benefit. Shipbuilding and commerce, integral parts of Boston's economy, employed hundreds of people who lived near the wharves, including ropewalk workers, carpenters, coopers, sailmakers, and "jack tars" or sailors. The well-being of many artisans and laborers was tied to overseas trade. Slowdowns in the port's activity, caused by wars or restrictive British policies, hurt everyone in Boston, from the wealthiest merchant to the most ordinary of workers.

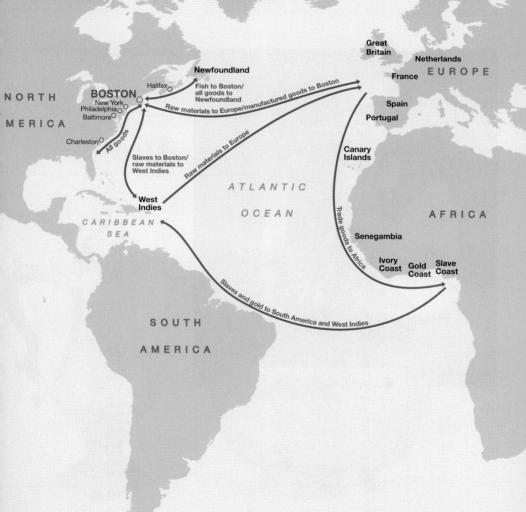

EUROPE

Great Britain

Netherlands

France

Spain

Portugal

Canary Islands

AFRICA

Senegambia

Ivory Coast

Gold Coast

Slave Coast

Trade goods to Africa

Slaves and gold to South America and West Indies

ATLANTIC

OCEAN

Newfoundland

Fish to Boston/all goods to Newfoundland

Raw materials to Europe/manufactured goods to Boston

Raw materials to Europe

BOSTON

Halifax

New York

Philadelphia

Baltimore

Charleston

All goods

Slaves to Boston/raw materials to West Indies

West Indies

CARIBBEAN SEA

NORTH AMERICA

SOUTH AMERICA

13

Boston was a provincial outpost, 3,000 miles from the center of the empire. With the growth of mercantile wealth in Massachusetts Bay, there arose a provincial class to patronize skilled artisans and, to a lesser extent, the fine arts. Together, successful merchants and governing officials set the style, their tastes imitative of London and reflecting the conviction that Europe was the source of culture and sophistication. Shopkeepers who specialized in luxury imports flourished in Boston. Booksellers, printsellers, and looking-glass sellers found buyers, disseminating ideas and styles through their wares. Boston supported dancing masters and music instructors. Engravers found work, and leading officials, traders, and clergymen sat to have their portraits painted. The products of Boston's many skilled luxury craftspeople were unsurpassed in British North America. They were produced, as their advertisements claimed, "in the neatest British manner" and the "latest" London styles. Housewrights, masons, carpenters, bricklayers, roofers, glaziers, paperhangers, and plasterers combined to build elaborate Georgian-style mansions for the wealthy. Cabinetmakers, carvers, upholsterers, japanners, chairmakers, and other craftsmen produced tea tables, card tables, settees, dining tables, chairs, and cabinet pieces to furnish the elite's parlors, dining rooms, and ballrooms. Silversmiths and goldsmiths, watchmakers and jewelers, custom tailors, skilled dressmakers, glovers, wigmakers—all found work in a culture that declared "luxuries" to be necessities for the socially ambitious.

John Singleton Copley's portrait of Paul Revere captures the talented artisan at about age 35 in work clothes at his work bench. Revere's skill as a silversmith is reflected in the coffeepot (below) *and in the "Liberty Bowl"* (below left) *honoring the 92 members of the Massachusetts Assembly who refused to rescind the Circular Letter protesting the 1767 Townshend Acts.*

numbered from one-half to two-thirds of the population. In some respects these craftspeople shared
experiences and aspirations. Few hoped to rise to the
level of the "better sort." Most sought to achieve a
life of modest comfort, free from debt. By luck and
diligence a man might serve an apprenticeship in his
youth, become a wage-earning journeyman in the
shop of an experienced craftsman, then gradually
save the capital to set up a shop of his own. As a master craftsman he would enjoy independence and control his own time and labor. He proudly wore the
leather apron that marked him as a skilled producer.
A few women—fashionable dressmakers, glovers,
and widows who managed to continue their husbands' trades—belonged to this class.

Yet only the fortunate could afford apprentice-
ships in the highly skilled, lucrative trades. For every
goldsmith or cabinetmaker, many more struggled
along as humble tailors, smiths, or shoemakers. Women in particular were concentrated in the ranks of
the lower trades: nurses, housekeepers, seamstresses.
They lived only narrowly above the classes beneath.
Among the "meaner sort" were laborers, including a
highly transient population of seamen and unskilled
workers, some of them the so-called "strolling poor,"
attracted from rural areas by the town's opportuni-
ties. Boston contained little indentured labor, but
roughly 800 townspeople were African American,
nearly all slaves and most working as household servants in 1765. Among the free population, some 30
percent qualified as poor or near poor: widows, seamen, laborers, and, when times were hard, minor artisans as well.

As the 18th century wore on, hard times became
common in Boston. Wealth was increasingly concentrated in the hands of those at the top of society,
while more people fell into the ranks of the impov-
erished. Even as men like John Rowe built mansions,
the plight of Boston was evident on the landscape:
some poor people lived in the town almshouse or the
brick workhouse on the Common, and many more—
nearly 1,000 in 1757—received outdoor (home)
relief. Of all the port towns in North America,
Boston alone stagnated in population and opportunity in the mid-1700s.

Part of the reason for Boston's decline lay in the
long and repeated wars that Britain waged with

All in a Day's Work on the Boston Waterfront

On a rough cobblestone street running to the wharf in the busy North End, Bostonians ply their trades. The time is 1769, a year after redcoated British soldiers were first quartered in town. There is a hustle and bustle to make the ship ready for a voyage to the West Indies. Ship riggers on the top mast (**1**) unfurl sails as cartmen (**2**) load barrels of rum and salted fish. A sail-

maker's helper (**3**) lowers a new sail on a winch from the sail-cloth loft where it has just been woven by the sailmaker (**4**). A blacksmith (**5**) forges iron bands for last-minute repairs to make the vessel seaworthy and a brazier (**6**) hammers new brass ship fittings. A merchant (**7**), in a stylish red coat of a gentleman complete with wig and cane, has come down to

the docks, very likely with last-minute instructions for the ship's captain. The seafaring men in the foreground are taking a break from work. A fisherman (**8**) leaning on his boat hook tells a joke that the fishmonger (**9**), resting his wooden shovel on a basket of fish, finds funny but the stern-faced seaman (**10**) doesn't get. Building tradesmen repair the porch roof of the

seamstress shop to the right: a master housewright (**11**) shouts orders to his journeyman (**12**), young apprentice (**13**), and laborer (**14**) while a carpenter (**15**) in leather apron shaves shingles. Leather aprons are the mark of tradesmen. A seamstress (**16**) in the doorway of her shop receives a lady's maid (**17**) bearing a garment from her mistress. A laundress (**18**) hauls buckets of water for her washtubs while two elderly market women (**19**) peddle a hot drink from their cart to a grenadier and battalion soldier from the British 29th Regiment of Foot (**20**). The lady's maid is among the 800 African Americans in Boston's "lower trades," which include the sailmaker's helper, the laborer on the roof, and the young porter (**21**) carrying a basket on his head. A newsboy (**22**) hawks the *Boston Gazette* to the merchant, a newspaper brimming with patriotic outrage against the redcoats that would erupt in March 1770 in the "Boston Massacre." The deceptively peaceful scene on the wharf is a lull before the storm.

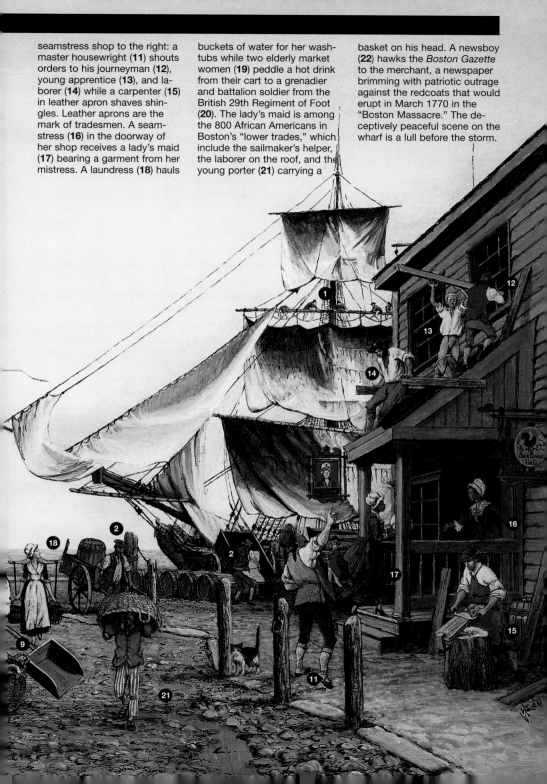

French settlements in North America. For some New Englanders, the wars provided profitable supply contracts, but in general they disrupted trade. They created widows and orphans, whose maintenance taxed the resources of the town.

Yet colonists generally embraced Britain's battles as their own. It was not just that economic opportunity seemed to lie within the empire. Equally important, as colonists saw it, liberty itself lay in the connection they had with Great Britain. When they fought against the French, they fought against papacy and an absolute monarchy as well as against a commercial rival. When they fought against France, they fought for the "rights of Englishmen."

Contemporaries did not entirely agree on just what those rights included. All were certain, however, that English rights derived from a proud history, from centuries of resistance by Englishmen against would-be tyrants and the gradual establishment of liberties for the lowly subjects. Harvard scholars, students at writing schools, readers of newspapers, and listeners who heeded either church sermons or tavern stories all learned this view of English history. Boston's lower classes showed their familiarity with the English heritage, too. They held popular celebrations every November 5, on the anniversary of Guy Fawkes's attempt in 1605 to blow up Parliament. On these "Pope's Days," crowds of petty artisans, apprentices, and laborers paraded about the streets, carrying effigies of the devil, the pope, and the Stuart pretender to the throne, a symbol of political absolutism. It was a day of disorder, which ended in a vigorous battle between companies from the North and South ends of town, each side trying to capture and burn the other's effigies. Boston's elite deplored the violent excesses of the day, but they accepted and even applauded the popular display of anti-popery and attachment to English history.

As New Englanders saw it, that history taught English people everywhere to treasure certain political institutions. English wars of the 17th century had established that the powers of the monarch would be countered by a sovereign Parliament, made up of a House of Lords and an elected House of Commons. Along with customary rights, such as trial by jury, this balanced structure of government protected England from both anarchy and tyranny. Massachusetts's government was modeled along the same lines. A royal governor, appointed by the king, held executive power. The colony had no House of Lords, but a Council, or upper house of the legislature, was filled with wealthy and educated gentlemen, nominated by the lower house and chosen by the governor. The lower house, called the Assembly, paralleled the English House of Commons, and was elected as representatives of the towns of the province. (Collectively, the Council and Assembly were known as the General Court.) Every year the Governor, Council, and Assembly met at the Old State House on State Street to decide matters of province-wide concern.

None of these institutions, it is important to note, was supposed to enact the will of the people. True, the representatives in the Assembly were elected by local town meetings, but even they were expected to transcend petty, local interest and promote the good of the whole province, not the advantage of their particular towns. Assemblymen were not as distinguished as Council members, but they were propertied and prominent well beyond the average. "A Gentleman of good natural Interest...a Man of Reading, Observation, and daily conversant with Affairs of Policy and Commerce, is certainly better qualified for a Legislator, than a Retailer of Rum and small Beer called a Tavern-keeper," wrote one commentator. Government, in the commonly held view of the day, belonged in the hands of the elite and "better sort."

Retailers of beer might have greater political voice in the institutions of local politics. At town meetings, usually held at Faneuil Hall, qualified voters—men with enough property—elected representatives, chose local officers, and regulated local affairs. Prominent men routinely filled town offices, but town meetings did allow broad participation. "Middling" interests organized small and self-selected caucuses, which met before the town meeting to choose slates of candidates and settle points of policy. By organizing in caucuses, the "middling" people sometimes outvoted the well-to-do.

Still other institutions protected the interests of the less powerful people. Ordinary voters served on juries, and juries were famous for refusing to convict the obviously guilty when officials tried to enforce unpopular laws. Able-bodied free men also served in

William Shirley, governor of Massachusetts, 1741-56. He organized the expedition that captured the French fortress of Louisbourg in 1745 and in 1749-53 served as a member of the commission meeting in Paris to determine the boundary line between New England and French North America. In 1755, he served briefly as commander in chief of British forces in North America after the death of Gen. Edward Braddock in the Battle of the Monongahela.

local militias that were supposed to keep the peace. New England militias were famous for failing to gather when local uprisings expressed widely-held grievances. With no professional police force and no standing army, popular discretion in law enforcement represented an important power. The system left space for ordinary people to decide whether or not to uphold the laws passed by gentlemen in the Council and Assembly. The people might even enforce their own moral standards without the blessing of government. Boston crowds broke open a private warehouse to seize scarce grain, tore down an unpopular marketplace, and attacked brothels. When they believed their vital interests were at stake, people among the lower ranks assumed a right to shape public policy. There was a recognized role for the people "out of doors"—outside the doors of the legislature and outside official positions of authority.

How far some Bostonians could take that principle appeared in the mid-1740s, in the distress of war and in the face of the Royal Navy itself. "Pressing" men into naval service was common in British ports, but in the colonies the legality of the practice was disputed. It was more than a fine legal question: impressment abrogated men's freedom and brought turmoil to an entire city. The "jack tars" and dockside workers who were seized understandably resented it, and everyone else in the port town also disliked the disruption of trade. News of a "hot press" at Boston deterred ships' captains from entering the harbor; even coasters with grain, fishing vessels, and small boatmen carrying firewood hesitated to sail to Boston.

In the fall of 1747, ships of the Royal Navy anchored in Boston, and some sailors took the opportunity to desert the service. To fill out his ships' complement, Com. Charles Knowles sent a press crew through the harbor. His officers seized nearly 40 seamen from trading ships in port and a few men who worked the waterfront. Boston exploded in a full three days of violent resistance. A crowd took Knowles's officers hostage, put the sheriff in the town stocks, and broke windows at the residence of Gov. William Shirley. Shirley summoned the militia, but they failed to muster. As the mob swelled into the thousands, Shirley fled for safety to Castle William, a fortification in the harbor. Peace was restored only when he negotiated with Knowles for the release of the impressed men.

In the aftermath of the riots, the Boston town meeting officially deplored the violence, saying that rioters had been "Foreign Seamen, Servants, Negroes, and other Persons of Mean and Vile Condition." But, in truth, a good many inhabitants had sympathized with the mob. Although they might disapprove of particular crowd actions, even the most conservative acknowledged the general principle that "mobs, a sort of them at least,...are constitutional." The mob was an institution that, however disorderly, was a recognized and necessary part of the way English people were ruled. Mobs stood alongside town meetings, jury trials, and the General Court in the framework of English government. Although gentlemen would govern in this system, and the propertied would direct affairs of the towns, their decisions would sometimes be vulnerable to the interests and beliefs of those beneath them in the social order.

When they celebrated British liberty or claimed the rights of Englishmen, what colonists often treasured most was this quality of government: that law was not—or not merely—handed down to ordinary subjects from above. It was not—or not easily—enforced against their wishes. Even petty artisans, sailors, and small farmers could make their own notions of right and justice felt. For many colonists, this was English liberty. It was what they defended against English authority beginning in the mid-1760s.

Prologue to Revolution

Printers were at the heart of revolutionary activities. From his shop near the Old State House, master printer Benjamin Edes published the news, both "foreign and domestic," in the weekly *Boston Gazette,* printed on a press like the one shown at left, used by his fellow printer, Isaiah Thomas. In his off-hours Edes joined other independent craftsmen to drink and socialize, to talk about politics, trade, or the latest local scandal. To the "better sorts," Edes and his associates were "mere mechanicks," but in the mid-1760s, they found themselves devising ways for the colonists to resist the will of Parliament. Within a few years, the *Gazette* would be known as "the weekly Dung Barge" among Boston "Tories," who deplored its opinionated articles in defense of colonial liberties. A handful of men—popular leaders Samuel Adams and Dr. Joseph Warren, and lawyers James Otis and John Adams—helped produce the paper, which one of them called "a curious employment." As they read and argued the issues of the *Gazette,* many Bostonians became part of a revolutionary movement.

It began with the matter of a little money. Britain hardly anticipated American outrage. From the English perspective, it seemed reasonable to help cover the costs of empire by taxing colonial trade. Following the mercantilist theory of the day, Parliament had regulated the trade of the empire since late in the 17th century. But some of these Navigation Acts had benefited colonial economies, and others had not been enforced anyway. Now, after a half-century of imperial conflict, France had been thoroughly routed from Canada. Britain stood as the dominant naval power of the North Atlantic. Its national debt, however, had grown to well over £100,000,000.

Two revenue-raising laws known as the Grenville Acts introduced turmoil. First, the Sugar Act of 1764 lowered the duty on French molasses from 6 pence per gallon to 3 pence, but it gave new powers to customs officers and made clear that the tax would actually be gathered. Then in 1765, Parliament passed a Stamp Act to tax newspapers, legal documents, and sundries such as dice and playing cards. Unconsulted by Parliament, colonists learned that ships carrying stamps were en route, and that England had appointed men among them to collect the stamp duty.

Printing presses such as Benjamin Edes's provided colonists with their first line of defense against these high-handed measures. In newspapers, pamphlets, and broadsides, colonists brought their grievances to the attention of their countrymen on both sides of the Atlantic. Bostonians had hoped that peace would bring economic recovery, re-opening the offshore fisheries and letting the merchant fleet take safely to the seas again. Now Parliament's policies threatened disaster. Even a threepenny tax made French molasses too costly, and without that commodity, trade to the West Indies would be put in jeopardy. "These regulations must break and subdue the hearts of traders here," said one of them. Sailors, mechanics, and lesser shopkeepers knew whose jobs would be

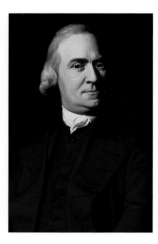

Samuel Adams appears in this painting by John Singleton Copley as a champion of the people demanding the expulsion of British troops in a town meeting in March 1770. Friend and foe considered him a principal organizer of resistance to British measures in caucuses, clubs, and committees as well as in the official town meeting and Massachusetts Assembly. He was a delegate to the Continental Congress and a signer of the Declaration of Independence. Thomas Jefferson called him "truly the man of the Revolution." His cousin, John Adams, described him as "a plain simple decent citizen, of middling stature, dress, and manners." Copley's portrait reflects that assessment.

lost, whose wages cut, and whose families pinched if the trade were seriously burdened. Political principles were also at stake. Lawyer James Otis boldly challenged British authority itself: By what right did Parliament, which contained no representatives elected by American colonists, presume to tax them? Other writers agreed that the laws were unfair. After all, the colonies had their own representative assemblies filled with local men who knew far better than Parliament what taxes the colonists could and could not bear.

In public taverns and at private firesides, Bostonians considered these ideas. Townspeople debated whether and how to resist the offensive laws. Benjamin Edes worried the matter with associates from his political caucus—a merchant, a ship's captain, two braziers, two distillers, a painter, and a jeweler—a group who called themselves "the Loyal Nine." Their decision became public on the morning of August 14, 1765. The town awoke to discover a stuffed effigy of the newly appointed stamp master, Andrew Oliver, hanging on a majestic elm tree in the South End. All day long nervous government officers dithered over whether to respond. In the evening, Bostonians of the "lower sort" moved into action. Ebenezer McIntosh, a poor shoemaker and captain of the South End Pope's Day company, led a crowd of many thousands to seize the effigy from the tree, parade it about the town, and triumphantly consign it to a bonfire. Some of the crowd attacked Oliver's house, breaking windows and furniture and trampling the garden. Next day, Oliver tentatively agreed not to distribute stamps. The stamps might arrive soon in Boston harbor, but there would be no one to take them in hand.

With popular action, Bostonians had effectively managed to block the law. Crowds in Rhode Island, Maryland, and Connecticut quickly followed Boston's lead. They made effigies of stamp masters, threatened violence, and demanded resignations. The methods themselves reflected the principles of liberty that were at stake. By their actions, crowds asserted the right to make popular notions of justice felt. In effect, colonists insisted that law should be made in American assemblies, American courts of law, and even American streets. It is a telling detail that, in December, when Andrew Oliver offered to resign at the Old State House, crowd leaders insisted he resign at what was now called the Liberty Tree instead. By resigning at that site, Oliver symbolically acknowledged the jurisdiction of the people out of doors.

Yet cooperation between respectable property owners, such as the Loyal Nine, and the "meaner sort" had its limits. Different ranks could agree that Parliament threatened their well-being, but poor Bostonians had broader grievances. Andrew Oliver's brother-in-law, Thomas Hutchinson, a rich merchant who served as lieutenant governor, became the next target of a Boston crowd. Despite initial objections to the Sugar and Stamp acts, Hutchinson felt duty-bound to uphold Parliament's right to tax. This stance, as well as his conspicuous wealth, ambition, and disdain for the "lower sorts," told against him in the turbulent summer of 1765. On the evening of August 26, a crowd attacked his stately mansion in the North End of town. It was no moderate or symbolic act. The mob broke windows, chopped down doors and interior walls, ransacked the merchant's possessions, drank his wine, and actually sawed off the cupola of his house. The destruction was shocking, even to many who had approved the coercion of stamp masters.

The Loyal Nine, joining with other townsmen as self-styled Sons of Liberty, quickly dissociated themselves from the riot at Hutchinson's house. Samuel Adams applauded the first crowd that forced Oliver's resignation but condemned the Hutchinson crowd as being of "a truly *mobbish* Nature." Such violent class hostility worried Adams, and it would alienate prosperous people of the town from resistance measures. The Sons of Liberty thus began the delicate project they would pursue over the next decade—to resist Parliament while restraining expressions of lower-class opinion. On this occasion they were lucky: political forces unrelated to the colonial dispute toppled the English ministry, and new leaders repealed the Stamp Act in 1766.

Officials announced the repeal from the balcony of the Old State House. Bostonians celebrated. They strung lanterns on the Liberty Tree, viewed an illuminated pyramid on Boston Common, and drank patriotic toasts. They had defended English liberty even against English authorities. They had managed an uneasy coalition between the town's propertied class and the lowly and disfranchised. Such a balance would prove difficult to keep.

James Otis Jr., the leading lawyer of colonial Boston, was famous for arguing against writs of assistance (arbitrary search warrants) on the grounds that every man's house is his castle. As the author of influential pamphlets attempting to define the rights of the colonies, he was a major political force in Boston until 1769, when a brutal caning by a British customs official caused him to lose his sanity. This 20th-century portrait of Otis by Robert S. Chase is reputedly based on 17th-century portraits by Joseph Blackburn and John Singleton Copley.

Thomas Hutchinson, a Boston-born and Harvard-educated merchant, had a long and varied public career in Massachusetts politics. His willingness to enforce the unpopular Grenville Acts while lieutenant governor and chief justice of the colony led to the ransacking of his house (left) during the Stamp Act riots in 1765. This 1741 portrait, the only known likeness, was painted by Edward Truman.

The Sugar Act and the Stamp Act

When Parliament passed the Sugar Act in 1764, it expected little opposition from the North American colonies. The act only enforced existing regulations on the Atlantic trade, and it actually lowered the tax on molasses imported from the French or Spanish West Indies. But Boston traders, who depended on the supply of foreign molasses, knew they would be hurt because lower duties, if actually collected, would be more onerous than higher duties that existed only in theory. The Sugar Act, with its rigorous enforcement policy, seemed designed to penalize North American

traders while giving a windfall to West Indies sugar planters. Boston merchants, fearing potential economic losses, objected to Parliament's favoring the interests of wealthy colonial planters above their own. In a town meeting at Faneuil Hall, Samuel Adams called the Act a flagrant violation of governmental authority and drafted a statement urging Massachusetts legislators to work to repeal it and join other colonies in opposition. Boston's response portended a more serious reaction if British policies continued to hurt colonial traders. The warning was confirmed by the response to

Parliament's passage of the Stamp Act in 1765 as colonists from Massachusetts to Georgia reacted with surprising unity. Representatives of eight continental colonies gathered in New York City at a Stamp Act Congress and protested the "Burdensome and grievous" tax on printed and legal documents. Other assemblies added their own petitions to Parliament. The reason why so many colonists shared a single opinion about the Stamp Act is symbolized by the Liberty Tree, which one historical account calls "the most common symbol of the American Revolu-

tion." In creating liberty trees, the colonists drew on long-standing English customs of the May Tree and the Maypole. Liberty trees expressed colonists' belief that their principles were rooted deep in the English past. As the patriots saw it, they were defending established and historical rights, not advancing innovative or radical theories. They felt justified by tradition in claiming that they should not be taxed without their consent. The common idea of long-standing English rights made it possible for colonists of different regions, beliefs, and interests to come to

gether to oppose the Stamp Act. Bostonians set the example when they displayed an effigy of their stamp distributor, Andrew Oliver *(left)*, on a large elm in the town's South End. Other towns established liberty trees or set up liberty poles on which they hoisted effigies *(below, left)*. During the next decade of mounting resistance to Parliamentary power, colonists conducted countless political parades, tarring and featherings, and other demonstrations at these sites.

John Adams called the Stamp Act an "enormous engine, fabricated by the British Parliament, for battering down all the rights and liberties of America." As England's first attempt to levy a direct tax on the colonists, it required that revenue stamps, such as the ones shown here, be placed on all commercial papers and legal documents, newspapers, pamphlets, cards, and dice. Printers felt particularly threatened by the act, since it imposed a halfpenny or penny tax, depending on size, on every newspaper copy sold and a shilling tax on every advertisement.

A LIST of the Names of *those*

who AUDACIOUSLY continue to counteract the UNIT-
ED SENTIMENTS of the BODY of Merchants thro'out
NORTH-AMERICA ; by importing British Goods
contrary to the Agreement.

John Bernard,
    (In King-Street, almost opposite Vern

James McMasters,
             (Or

Patrick McMasters,
        (Opposite th

John Mein,
    (Opposite the White-Hors

Nathaniel Rogers,
    (Opposite Mr. Henderson In
    King-Street.

William Jackson,
    At the Brazen Head, Cornhill, n

Theophilus Lillie,
    (Near Mr. Pemberton's Meeting-

John Taylor,
    (Nearly opposite the Heart and Crow

Ame & Elizabeth Cummings,
(Opposite the Old Brick Meeting House, all of Boston.

Israel Williams, Esq; & Son,
    (Traders in the Town of Hatfield.

And, *Henry Barnes,*
    (Trader in the Town of Marlboro'.

---

*The following Names should have been inserted in
the List of Justices.*

County of Middlesex.	County of Lincoln.
Samuel Hendley	
John Borland	John Kingsbury
Henry Barnes	
Richard Cary	County of Berkshire.
County of Bristol.	Mark Hopkins
George Brightman	Elijah Dwight
County of Worcester.	Israel Stoddard
Daniel Bliss	

New Controversies 1766–70

To force Britain to change its policies, patriots adopted a boycott of British imports. In Boston the names of merchants who refused to go along with the non-importation agreement were printed in the newspapers, on a leaflet, and in the *North American Almanac* (1770). Betsy and Anne Cuming, listed ninth and spelled "Cummings" on the blacklist *(left)*, were orphans, sisters who kept a small shop and sold imported linens just to get by. "It was verry triffling, owr Business," wrote Betsy *(inset)*, but the sisters faced a disapproving patriot committee who asked them to close up shop. By the late 1760s, the movement begun by the Sons of Liberty had reached small retailers like the Cuming sisters. Was it necessary to the patriot cause "to inger two industrious Girls who ware Striving in an honest way to Git there Bread"? As the quarrel with England escalated, some people in Boston thought that it was.

Bostonians had celebrated their good fortune too soon. In 1767, they learned of a new set of Parliamentary regulations, formed by Chancellor of the Exchequer Charles Townshend, and designed to raise revenue directly from the colonial trade. The Townshend Acts laid duties on tea, glass, paper, and painters' colors. Equally important, they appointed a Board of Customs to oversee incoming cargoes and collect the duties owed. Although the five commissioners named to the board would hardly be able to police the harbors all along the coast to Georgia, they were sufficient to hinder trade in Boston, where they were headquartered.

In response, colonists again turned to the press to assess their situation and prescribe its remedy. Many read articles written by "A Farmer in Pennsylvania" —really John Dickinson—as he frankly denied Parliament's right to enact colonial laws. Just as obnoxious in the eyes of patriot pamphleteers were the new customs commissioners, denounced as mere hirelings paid to enforce the unpopular law. These officers would put money into their pockets every time that they—rightly or wrongly—seized a ship's cargo for the Crown. Such a system rewarded officials for being petty, intrusive, and careless of traders' rights.

Early in 1768, the Massachusetts Assembly addressed a circular letter to the assemblies of the other colonies, listing grievances and calling for joint action. An outraged King George III demanded that the Assembly rescind the obnoxious letter. Assembly members voted, 92 to 17, not to back down. Throughout the province, patriots toasted the faithful and virtuous 92 and roundly condemned the 17 rescinders. Francis Bernard, Royal governor of Massachusetts, followed the instructions of his superiors and dissolved the session of the General Court.

With the provincial Assembly unable to meet, opposition to the Townshend regulations fell to local town meetings and to informal and sometimes mob-bish assemblies. The Sons of Liberty became active again. They devised another powerful form of resistance. In 1764, some merchants had decided not to import British manufactures. They put aside laces, ruffles, and other expensive finery, so as to offset their debts and renew their own virtue. Facing the Townshend Acts in 1767, patriots extended this idea of boycotting trade. The Boston town meeting circulated a pledge to inhabitants. Signers agreed not to buy British goods, consume imported luxuries, or do business with dealers who did stock imports. At the same time they would encourage American manufactures. They would patronize colonial artisans, purchase homespun from local countrywomen, and leave off eating lamb so as to increase supplies of wool. The idea spread through the colonies.

As a political tactic, the boycotts offered three main advantages. By cutting off trade, patriots hoped to trim the profits of British merchants and manufacturers, who in turn might lobby English authorities to repeal objectionable laws. Although they were not represented in Parliament, colonists could still have an impact on Englishmen who were.

A second advantage lay closer to home. Writers and clergymen claimed that stopping unnecessary imports would benefit American society. Doing without the luxuries of Britain would make the colonists more self-reliant. The pacts called on individuals to sacrifice for the common good, to wean themselves from consumption, and adopt what Abigail Adams called a "Simplicity of Manners." As colonists became frugal and virtuous, they would secure their liberties.

Third, the non-importation and non-consumption agreements called on almost everyone to participate. Merchants' cooperation was essential; the wealthy John Hancock, John Rowe, and others lined up on the patriot side. At the same time, tradesmen, laborers, and farmers all actively policed the pacts. Even those unqualified to vote in town meeting had a role, for men with limited property and women of most classes could sign an agreement not to deal in British goods or patronize traders who did. As consumers and manufacturers, women were essential participants in the resistance effort. This new involvement of women—who could not vote and who were rarely asked their political opinion—made the patriots' movement startlingly inclusive.

In the late 1760s, a flurry of activity ensued. At Harvard College, students wore homespun to graduation ceremonies. The well-to-do renounced fancy mourning dress at funerals. Calling themselves "daughters of liberty," women met privately in ministers' homes and publicly on the Common to produce thread for homespun. More than 300 Boston matrons signed a pledge to renounce that fashionable beverage, tea. Eleven-year-old Anna Green Winslow recorded in her diary, "As I am (as we say) a daughter of liberty I chuse to wear as much of our own manufactory as pocible." Even young girls might find a political role.

But while the boycott offered many Bostonians a welcome opportunity to defend American liberties, it was an unwelcome imposition on others. People held mixed views on the imperial controversy. It was perfectly possible to deplore Parliament's law but also deplore some of the *Gazette's* opinions, the Sons' tactics, or the violent mobbing of Hutchinson's house. Now it became hard to straddle the fence. Whether you bought imported cloth or dressed in homespun, attended tea parties or refused to go, patronized importers like the Cuming sisters or shopped somewhere else—these decisions declared a political allegiance. Once Andrew Oliver had stood alone before the Liberty Tree, pressured into resigning as stamp master; now many other Bostonians felt pushed—even stampeded—into embracing the patriot cause in a public forum. Those who hesitated faced harangues from their more fervent neighbors. Storekeepers, innkeepers, and dealers of all kinds found that they could comply with the patriot program or face ostracism, incivility, and possible ruin.

The boycotts, then, had a double effect. They were a critical unifying force. They brought together Bostonians high and low, male and female, young and old. They united seaports with the countryside. At the same time, however, non-importation tactics sharply divided colonists from one another. Small retailers pointed out that they lacked the capital and stock on hand to withstand even a temporary stop in trade. The Cuming sisters did not see how they could close their little business, for "that littil we must do to enabel us to Support owr family." Meanwhile, wealthy

Anna Green Winslow, a girl of 10 when she came to Boston in 1770 to live with her aunt and uncle, kept a diary for her parents in Nova Scotia. She attended school to learn reading, writing, and sewing, read books, including Pilgrim's Progress *and Gulliver's Travels, and went to dancing assemblies. She was politicized by the movement among women to spin and weave American cloth, calling herself "a daughter of liberty." She died of sickness in the fall of 1779 in her 21st year. The artist who painted this portrait of her is unknown.*

Francis Bernard, seen here in a 1767 portrait by John Singleton Copley, was royal governor of New Jersey before being transferred to Massachusetts in 1760. While not unsympathetic to colonial grievances, he was too loyal to the Crown to disobey orders. By 1769 Bernard's strict enforcement of unpopular ministry measures had so angered Bostonians that the British government was forced to recall him in an attempt to calm an explosive situation. His replacement, Thomas Hutchinson, fared no better and later shared a similar fate.

merchants could use non-importation as a means to undo small competitors. Self-interest also divided artisans, since some trades flourished in the protected home market while others stagnated. Finally, the harassment faced by importers alienated many of them irrevocably. Some people gloried in being friends to the cause, others were branded "enemies to the liberties of their country."

Importers were not the only ones to encounter coercive tactics. Customs commissioners, enforcement officers, and informers were starkly unpopular in town. The regulations they enforced were complicated and annoying at best. Even worse, the men chosen for the posts were haughty, malicious, and more than a little greedy. They practiced what one historian has called "customs racketeering," seizing ships on technicalities and taking a full one-third of the total value of every vessel they condemned. They proceeded with little fear of legal consequences; contests over their behavior were resolved in admiralty courts, without a local jury. To check these officials' and informers' excesses would take a Boston crowd.

Indeed, in June 1768, a crowd did the job. Once again, a combination of grievances fueled the patriot movement. For several weeks officers from the warship *Romney* offended town workingmen by impressing civilians into the crew. Patriot leaders had discouraged crowd action: "No Mobs or Tumults," proclaimed the *Gazette*. Then, customs men seized John Hancock's sloop *Liberty*. True enough, Hancock had not entered bond for his cargo as the law required, but, as the commissioners well knew, the general practice was to do so just before sailing. It seemed a trumped-up charge. With warships in the harbor, angry dock workers and seamen could not prevent the seizure, but they could and did bloody some of the commissioners and destroy some of their property.

In the wake of this riot, four of the customs commissioners fled for safety to Castle William. They could only look out from the battlements at the ships they were supposed to be regulating. For some months, Governor Bernard had been writing authorities in England, insisting that the Townshend laws could not be enforced in Boston without military backing. Now the commissioners added their plea for troops. Bostonians were a lawless rabble, they said, and loyal officers such as themselves could not walk the streets for fear of their lives. Over the summer the British ministry accepted their point of view, and England dispatched four regiments to restore order to the disobedient port of Boston.

On October 1, a subdued populace watched as 12 ships of war in the harbor turned broadsides to the shore, as if ready to fire upon the town. The first two regiments—700 men—had arrived. They marched up the Long Wharf along King Street to the Common, their scarlet coats brilliant in the fall air, their fifes and drums resounding through the streets.

Boston became a garrisoned town, flooded with Regulars as the two final regiments arrived. The troops were there, the patriots insisted, "to awe and terrify" the inhabitants. Samuel Adams, his cousin John, and a handful of others led the effort to prove that the troops were unnecessary. The town kept decent order, and the ministry returned half the troops to Halifax, Nova Scotia, in the summer of 1769. Meanwhile, *A Journal of The Times* rolled off Benjamin Edes's printing press every week, reporting the hardships of military occupation to readers in New York and Philadelphia. Townspeople now woke to the roll of drums and the clank of bayonets. Upstanding inhabitants going home at night were challenged by armed sentries in their own streets. Some of the soldiers were raucous, some were habitually "in liquor." Respectable women were insulted in the streets, and military drills interrupted the meditations of churchgoers on the Sabbath.

Besides, as John Adams noted, the soldiers ultimately proved "wretched" peacekeepers. Forbidden to act without the request of a civil magistrate, they could only stand idly by many street disorders. Take, for example, what happened to John Mein, a printer as loyal to Parliament as Ben Edes was to the people. Mein's paper, *The Boston Chronicle,* nagged the patriots for months. Mein boldly scoffed at non-importation schemes and claimed that leading patriots secretly cheated on them. His offenses eventually aroused a patriot crowd. Betsy Cuming overheard the melee. There was "a voilint Skreeming Kill him Kill him," she recalled, and Mein narrowly eluded a group of Sons of Liberty. The printer later escaped to the *Romney* and sailed for England. That same evening another crowd of the "lower sort" seized a

Next pages: *Two regiments of British infantry from Halifax, Nova Scotia, disembark from their ships on their way to Boston's Long Wharf on October 1, 1768, to maintain order and enforce the customs laws. Paul Revere characterized their subsequent march up King Street as an "insolent parade."*

Braintree lawyer John Adams gained local prominence in 1765 as a leading opponent of the Stamp Act. In 1770, he agreed, from a sense of duty, to help defend Capt. Thomas Preston and the British soldiers charged with murder in what Samuel Adams and other radicals were calling "the Boston Massacre." Many patriots considered him a traitor to the cause of liberty. This portrait by Benjamin Blyth shows Adams in about 1766.

known customs informer and tarred and feathered him in the street.

Despite the presence of British soldiers, such incidents multiplied. Early in 1770, Sons of Liberty organized apprentices and schoolboys to picket the store of importer Theophilus Lillie. Ebeneezer Richardson, a customs informer, tried to disperse the crowd. The boys shouted him down and chased him off, throwing stones until the unhappy man reached the door of his own house. A moment later, Richardson appeared at an upstairs window and fired a gun into the street below. Eleven-year-old Christopher Seider, son of a German immigrant, fell dead. At the boy's funeral, patriots staged a massive, peaceful demonstration. Thousands of women and men flanked the way to the graveside and marched in mourning. A child had been killed on Boston streets, amidst the very troops supposed to keep order. Many argued that the soldiers' presence had made things worse, for it had emboldened men like Richardson.

It was only a matter of time before the troops themselves became embroiled. The city's workingmen had particular reasons to resent the soldiery. On their off-hours, some soldiers took jobs to supplement their wages. Already suffering in economic recession, laboring men were in no mood to be done out of a job by an off-duty "lobsterback." In early March, a soldier passed John Gray's ropewalk. Did he want a job, asked a journeyman ropeworker? Yes. Then perhaps he could clean the ropeworker's privy. Insults turned to blows. When the soldier rounded up his fellows at a nearby barracks, a street brawl ensued. It lasted hours, until John Gray himself arrived and restored an uneasy peace.

Three days later, angry workingmen and soldiers faced each other again, at the now famous event of March 5, the Boston Massacre on King Street. Contemporaries collected many eyewitness accounts, and others testified at a trial at law, but events were chaotic, memories differed, and what actually happened remains far from certain. We know that a crowd gathered on the icy street, shouting, gesticulating, throwing snowballs and rocks at the sentry at the custom house, across from the Old State House. The officer of the day, Captain Thomas Preston of the 29th Regiment of Foot, took a guard of seven men and bravely threaded through the mob to aid the sentry. There was a sudden flash of powder and a volley of shots. Within minutes, three men lay dead on the street. Two others, mortally wounded, would die within days. The list of victims makes clear that workingmen filled the crowd: Samuel Maverick, apprentice to an ivory turner; Patrick Carr, apprentice leather breeches maker; James Caldwell and Crispus Attucks, sailors; Samuel Gray, worker at the ropewalk.

Months later, a Boston jury cleared Captain Preston of ordering the carnage and settled guilt on the only two soldiers fairly certain to have fired their guns and caused deaths. John Adams, as lawyer for the soldiers, denounced the rioters as a "motley rabble of saucy boys, negroes and molattoes, Irish teagues and outlandish jack tarrs." Nevertheless, the loss of life at the "Horrid and Bloody Massacre" shocked the town. Patriot leaders, who had discouraged confrontation with the troops, now made use of its occurrence. Samuel Adams rallied the town meeting that packed into Old South Meeting House. The town demanded immediate removal of the troops and held firm until the Governor complied. The age-old British principle had been established in Boston: "Military power is created by civil communities to protect not to govern them." But it had been at the cost of human life and considerable weakening of Britain's hold on Boston's loyalties.

The Boston Massacre

For more than two centuries, Paul Revere's print of the Boston Massacre of March 5, 1770 *(opposite page)*, has shaped Americans' idea of that dramatic event. Revere copied (without permission) from a work by Boston artist Henry Pelham. Rushed into print, Revere's image made a strong and timely political point. Judged by evidence given at the soldiers' trials and by other eyewitnesses, Revere's version distorted the event in several respects. He depicted unarmed townspeople, well-dressed and peaceable. He portrayed the soldiers drawn up in an orderly line, firing into the crowd at the command of their captain. A Boston jury found that the redcoats had fired their weapons in a confused manner, not on any officer's orders. Besides, the crowd was distinctly less well-to-do than Pelham and Revere showed it to be. It was composed of working people, some of whom carried clubs and pelted the soldiers with rocks and snowballs. The patriot depiction misrepresented events to win sympathy and support from people outside Boston. Even at the time, not everyone accepted the patriot view. John Adams, who served as a defense lawyer for the soldiers, dismissed the crowd in King Street as a "motley rabble of saucy boys, negroes and molattoes, Irish teagues and outlandish jack tarrs." Historians note that the massacre fol-

The print above shows the 14th and 29th regiments of British troops landing at the Long Wharf in 1768 in response to the rioting that had broken out over a series of repressive revenue measures enacted by the English parliament. It was "Engraved, Printed, & Sold by Paul Revere," who used it for both financial and political purposes. Right: *A soldier of the 29th Regiment of Foot.*

lowed on the heels of seemingly petty disputes. A few days earlier, ropewalk workers had brawled with soldiers in the streets. On March 5, a fracas arose when a wigmaker's apprentice taunted a British captain over a disputed barber bill. Patriots might have seen the resulting encounter as a grievous case of British oppression, but from another view it seemed a tragic but petty incident. Many 18th-century Americans found it impossible to separate the two views. Daily conflicts were just what they expected when government stations an armed force amidst a civilian population. Over the centuries, Englishmen had struggled to ensure that no monarch would rule them with a standing army. Bostonians knew that the ministry currently ruled and taxed Ireland by an armed force. In fact, two of the four regiments sent to Boston in 1768 came directly from Irish duty. Although violence might break out over seemingly small matters, there was nothing trivial about the fundamental issue in the minds of many Bostonians: would colonists in British North America be reduced to the oppressed position of the Irish or retain the status of free English subjects? The massacre raised questions of principle that were fundamental to the Revolution. The Declaration of Independence had no less than four clauses touching on the dangers of "standing armies." The Constitution and Bill of Rights enshrine civilian supremacy over the military, the right to a fair trial, and freedom of assembly. America's founding documents were profoundly influenced by the bloody conflict of March 5, 1770.

Trouble Brewing

Dramatic events often grow out of small acts of ordinary people. One such event, the tarring and feathering of customs official John Malcolm in January 1774, is depicted in the British engraving at left. It was precipitated when shoemaker George Robert Twelves Hewes attempted to stop Malcolm from caning a little boy on a Boston street and was himself beaten. A crowd seized Malcolm, who had a reputation for informing on shipowners smuggling cargo and on sailors who smuggled in a few bottles of liquor, rolled him in tar and feathers, and carted him through the streets. The incident occurred a few weeks after the Tea Party, and the cartoonist has taken liberties, combining the events. Bostonians in the background are throwing tea into the harbor while the men in the foreground are pouring tea down Malcolm's throat. The Stamp Act hangs upside down on the Liberty Tree, symbol of patriot resistance. Patriot leaders favored organized actions such as dumping the tea, but opposed random acts like this one that they could not control, using the slogan "No violence or you'll hurt the cause."

Two years of military occupation, capped by the shock of the Massacre in King Street, had left townspeople sobered and unsettled. When the troops departed in 1770, Boston breathed a collective sigh of relief that the redcoats were gone. Townspeople began to reclaim their streets, wharves, and daily lives.

English authorities helped the process with compromise measures. Parliament repealed most of the Townshend Acts. The ministry made peace with the Massachusetts General Court by allowing Governor Bernard to call the legislature back into session, ignoring the Assembly's offensive 1768 circular letter of grievances. The duty on tea remained, and the Board of Customs Commissioners still sat in Boston to enforce it. Some patriots thought that these grievances should still be contested, but most colonists were tired of conflict. Overseas merchants longed to return to business. When traders in New York City decided to abandon the boycott agreement, merchants everywhere scrambled to reopen British trade. Boston, too, let the constitutional issues subside.

Still, the events of the previous years were not easily forgotten. On the surface, life in the seaport resumed a familiar pattern in the early 1770s. Beneath the surface, people remained wary of English intentions. No one rested secure in their membership in the glorious empire. No one could unreservedly celebrate the liberty ensured by their status as British colonials. The implications of their experience worked their way into people's minds and hearts.

One change lay in Bostonians' new connections with their fellow colonists, whether in Massachusetts or the distant Carolinas. Since the Stamp Act, patriot leaders had learned the tactical value of forming coalitions. The Sons of Liberty had built an informal network throughout the colonies. The Assembly had appealed to other provinces' legislatures. Under military occupation, the city had received sympathy and

In her poems and plays published in Boston, Mercy Otis Warren enlisted women in the patriot cause. In a poem supporting the boycott of British imports, she pleaded with women to put "female ornaments aside." In one of her plays she satirized Gov. Thomas Hutchinson, Justice Peter Oliver, and other Tories. In another she celebrated female heroines in the struggle for freedom in other countries. In 1805 she published a three-volume history of the Revolution, the first such by a woman. Her brother, James Otis, and husband, James Warren, were both prominent patriot leaders. This portrait by John Singleton Copley shows Mrs. Warren in her home in Plymouth.

support from people in other colonies. Bostonians discovered common ground with planters in Virginia, farmers in Connecticut, and traders in Philadelphia, New York, and Charleston. From that discovery colonists took a new vision of themselves. They began to shape an identity less English, more American.

When a new challenge to their rights appeared, then, Boston patriots relied on unity with others. In 1772, Thomas Hutchinson, now governor of the province, announced that the Royal Treasury, fed by customs revenue, would pay his own salary and the salaries of the judges of the superior court. It was a break for taxpayers but also a threat to liberty. Royal officers had depended on the elected Assembly for salaries. Armed with economic independence, those officers could execute unpopular policies without hesitation.

Alarmed, the Boston town meeting adopted a proposal by Samuel Adams. It named a Committee of Correspondence to compose an account of colonial rights and grievances and sent it to other Massachusetts towns, asking for "a free communication of their Sentiments" in return. As a way to mobilize unified resistance, the idea was a master stroke. Thousands gathered in town meetings to consider Boston's message. More than 100 towns appointed corresponding committees and sent replies to the capital. Most opposed the salary law. "All civil officers are or ought to be servants to the people and dependent upon them for their official Support," wrote Braintree's committee. Whatever their precise language in this case, the committees stood ready to protest all future provocation. Boston, whose ties to England now seemed a source of oppression, found security in new ties with inland communities.

Patriots also reexamined the social ties that linked Bostonians to one another. Colonists had always known that their society differed from England. There were rich and poor in Massachusetts, but no hereditary aristocrats with immense fortunes. A few of the "better sort" of colonists had even suggested that establishing an American aristocracy would be a good idea. Now it seemed that maybe England's historic balance among monarchy, aristocracy, and gentry was not the best bulwark of liberty after all. Perhaps the more egalitarian social structure of Massachusetts Bay was better. Most colonists surely did not desire an aristocracy. Besides, in the conflict with Parliament, petty tradesmen and farmers were proving as virtuous and patriotic as the high and mighty. Some people began to question the commonplace belief that those with social station were the proper leaders of government and society.

In this atmosphere, the city's deepest social inequalities came under attack. In 1767, the Boston town meeting instructed its representatives to outlaw the slave trade. In other towns, too, some patriots reconsidered their acceptance of bondage. African Americans quickly saw the implications of patriot rhetoric, and some allied with the patriot cause. Crispus Attucks, killed by a bullet at the Boston Massacre, was an African-American sailor. His other appearance in the historical record was in 1750, when one William Brown of Framingham advertised that his slave Attucks had run away. Though we know little else about him, these two acts—Attucks's bid for personal freedom and his presence in a King Street mob hostile to the authority of redcoats—suggest that white patriots had little to teach African Americans about the value of freedom. Phillis Wheatley, the brilliant young African-American poet, expressed her political sympathies in poems composed "On the death of Master Seider" and "On the affray in King Street." In a letter to a Mohegan Indian friend, she also wrote, "God has implanted a Principle, which we call love of Freedom; it is impatient of Oppression, and Pants for Deliverance.... I will assert that the same Principle lives in us." Most patriots' opposition to slavery was limited in the 1770s, but new thinking about the institution had begun.

The trend toward social and political change worried some of the "better sort." Ordinary men and women had become involved in the politics of the province and the empire. Circulation of the *Boston Gazette* rose swiftly from roughly 500 subscribers to near 2,000; the even more radical *Massachusetts Spy* had a subscription rate of 3,500 by 1775. More people participated in town meetings, and even men unentitled to the vote pressed for a voice. In place of town meetings, meetings of the whole "body of the people" consulted in Old South Meeting House. Artisans in particular grew politically assertive, pressing their social superiors toward more radical and egali-

Next pages: Samuel Adams addresses an overflow crowd assembled in the Old South Meeting House on December 16, 1773, to protest the British tax on tea and debate the fate of several tea ships then anchored in Boston harbor. With an estimated 5,000 people in attendance, it was the largest meeting ever held in the city. From it came the famous Boston Tea Party at Griffin's Wharf.

John Hancock was not yet 30 years old when he inherited his uncle's business and became Boston's richest man in 1764. He owned a gold snuffbox engraved with the likeness of George III that the king had given him on a visit to London. Hancock commissioned John Singleton Copley to paint this portrait and the one of Samuel Adams (page 24). He hung them both in his parlor as a message to Tories of his commitment to the patriot cause.

tarian thinking. Some people, like Thomas Hutchinson, would not compromise. Yet to lead the patriot movement—even to take part in it at all—prominent Bostonians had to accept changes in the social and political order. They had to consult the opinions of artisans and even lowly laboring men. They had to create unity across lines of class as well as region.

By the end of 1773, the town would need all the unity it could muster. In May, Parliament passed the Tea Act, meant not to open colonial disputes but to assist an ailing English corporation, the East India Company. The Tea Act let the company appoint its own agents in the American colonies to sell directly at retail. It seemed possible that consumers would welcome the change. Without middlemen or onerous taxes, company agents would be able to offer tea at a very low price. But American merchants were hardly pleased to be cut out of the tea business altogether. Were they to stand idly by as a handful of hand-picked agents monopolized the entire tea trade? Besides, those chosen as company agents were an offensive lot: among them, ready to profit, were Thomas Hutchinson's two sons.

Parliament reaped the harvest of the suspicions sown in the crises of the previous decade. Many Americans—even those who stood to enjoy cheaper tea—interpreted the Tea Act as a step toward their oppression. The act would lodge control in a very few hands. Once it had a monopoly on tea, once it had run other merchants out of business, what was to prevent the East India Company from raising prices to extravagant heights? What was to stop Parliament from raising the tax on tea to offset the treasury debt? Americans so distrusted Parliament that these developments seemed likely.

Once again colonists coordinated their response across provincial borders. In New York, Charleston, Philadelphia, and elsewhere, crowds of citizens met tea ships as they arrived in port and urged the captains not to unload but return the cargo to England. But the plan failed in Boston. Three ships laden with East India Company tea docked at Griffin's Wharf. Governor Hutchinson refused to allow the ships to leave the harbor without unloading.

Patriots were in a quandary: once the tea was ashore in warehouses or shops around the city, preventing sales would be difficult. Bostonians might be virtuous, but too many doted on tea to pass it up entirely. It would be far easier to resist it in a single, public gesture. The crisis brought townspeople en masse to a public meeting on November 29. Faneuil Hall held some 1,200 people, but so many packed in that the gathering adjourned to Old South Meeting House, which could accommodate many more. More than official voters, "the whole body of the people" took part. Over the next two weeks, mass meetings at Old South tried to resolve the crisis. Emissaries asked Hutchinson one last time to reship the tea. When Hutchinson refused, Samuel Adams reportedly concluded the December 16 meeting with the famous words: "This meeting can do nothing more to save the country."

It was the signal for others to act. There arose a hubbub outside Old South, and a motley tribe of "Mohawks" flocked to Griffin's Wharf. As George Robert Twelves Hewes recounted, some appeared in elaborate Indian disguises, others hastily blackened their faces with coal dust. More than 100 men divided into three companies, climbed aboard the tea ships, and set to work. Within three hours they emptied £9,000 worth of cargo into the cold water of the harbor. Thousands stood as spectators along the quayside.

Historians doubt Hewes's claim that John Hancock was present at the so-called Tea Party. Most participants were workingmen, with the know-how and physical strength to upend and break open large crates of cargo. Besides, it was part of the plan for leaders like Hancock to be conspicuously innocent someplace else in town. But elite patriots did support the workingmen on the wharf. In one sense, Hewes was right: men like Hancock "were there." For humble people like Hewes, once tongue-tied around his betters, things were changing. Hewes could convince himself that he was working shoulder to shoulder with the likes of John Hancock. More and more patriots saw it and felt it happening: a certain equality was becoming part of their movement for liberty. That development gave some people pause. It gave others a vital stake in pressing the resistance to its logical end.

George Robert Twelves Hewes, a shoemaker, was a man who ordinarily would not have had his portrait painted. But it was painted in 1835 by Joseph Cole when Hewes was in his 90s and Bostonians believed him to be one of the last surviving members of the Tea Party. He had also been present when townspeople confronted British troops on March 5, 1770, in what became known as the Boston Massacre. During the Revolution he served as both soldier and sailor, and British troops destroyed his small shop. He left town during the British occupation and never lived in Boston again. When he visited Boston in 1835, he was honored as a hero at the Fourth of July celebration.

The Tea Party

When a band of colonists picked up tea chests like the one at right and emptied their contents into the cold water of Boston harbor on December 16, 1773, it was both a pragmatic and a symbolic act. In practical terms, the Tea Party *(shown below in a contemporary engraving)* resolved a political stalemate. Colonists objected to the Tea Act, which gave the East India Company a monopoly on sales of tea. During the fall, patriots stopped ships carrying company tea from unloading. In many port cities, they persuaded the ships' captains to return their controversial cargo to England. Boston's patriot leaders hoped to do the same. But Massachusetts's Royal governor, Thomas Hutchinson, steadfastly refused to allow the three tea ships in harbor to sail. Mass meetings of patriots in Old South Meeting House stubbornly insisted that the tea not be unloaded. Neither side budged. Destroying the tea was a practical—though provocative—solution to the stand-off. The Tea Party also contained

symbolic elements. The majority of participants that night blackened their faces with soot, like members of English crowds often did. As patriots frequently said, they were defending the "rights of Englishmen." But some of the patriots on Griffin's Wharf dressed to resemble American Indians. This decision seems to express a change in the way some patriots saw their movement. To dress as "Mohawks" was to choose distinct-ly American garb. The costume referred to the New World instead of the Old. This new emphasis appeared in other forms as well. By the early 1770s, patriot writers were speaking less about English history and English rights and more about the "natural rights" that belonged to all men. On both sides of the Atlantic, engravers drew cartoons about the imperial conflict, depicting British North America as an Indian maiden and England as a mature and fashionable European lady. These images made a clear contrast between Old World and New. America was characterized by youth and simplicity; England by age and artificiality. Taken together, these indicators reflected a new direction; patriots now looked less to the English past, more to an American future.

"Now We are Enemies"

Paul Revere is best known to Americans of later generations as the horseman who spread the news of British troops to Lexington in April 1775. In his own time, he was best known as a silversmith and an engraver—skilled, successful, and highly gregarious. Popular among his fellow craftsmen, familiar with elite and humble alike, Revere organized resistance among the mechanics of the North End. His engravings of "the Bloody Massacre" and "The Landing of the Troops" circulated widely in the colonies, depicting the British as aggressors and Bostonians as brave defenders of colonial liberties. He helped to spread patriot ideas by other means, too: by horseback and carriage, he carried copies of town resolves and political intelligence to patriot networks out of town. In April 1775, he delivered a critical message to Lexington, warning that British troops had loaded their muskets and were on the march. Today, Cyrus Dallin's equestrian statue of Revere (*left*), silhouetted against the spires of the Old North Church, honors the Boston patriot.

Parliament responded to the Tea Party with forceful measures, a series of laws fittingly called "The Coercive Acts," dubbed the Intolerable Acts by patriots. They declared the port of Boston closed to all trade and dispatched the Royal Navy to ensure that no ships sailed in or out of the harbor. Boston must make restitution to the owners of the tea and show subordination to Parliament.

At the same time, British officials dramatically altered the Massachusetts government. Frustrated governors had been urging reforms for more than a decade. Britain now tried to limit the power of popular institutions and increase executive power. Henceforth, Parliament ruled. The royal governor, not the Assembly, would choose members of the Council. The local institution that had promoted so many patriot activities, the town meeting, was outlawed, except for an annual meeting to elect officers. There were to be no more gatherings where "the very dregs of the people" could frustrate the will of Parliament.

Other Coercive Acts reformed the course of justice in the colony. Now sheriffs would select all jurymen, and a customs official or crown officer accused of a crime in the colonies could escape the ill-temper of the populace and go to England or Nova Scotia for trial. A new and more fearsome military force—11 full regiments—would enforce these measures in Boston. Lt. Gen. Thomas Gage, commander of all British forces in America, would replace Thomas Hutchinson as governor. Taken together, these laws changed every major institution of colonial government. They aimed at defusing resistance once and for all by closing down the arenas in which people had debated, mobilized, and communicated with one another.

News of the Coercive Acts divided Bostonians. Many merchants favored conciliation. Shocked by the mob's destruction of private property at Griffin's Wharf, some moderates urged the town to make

Lt. Gen. Thomas Gage, British commander in chief in North America and the last royal governor of Massachusetts. After patriot forces surrounded Boston following the battle of Lexington and Concord, he imposed martial law in the city, proclaiming all rebels traitors. He did, however, offer to pardon those who would peacefully lay down their arms—except Samuel Adams and John Hancock. The costly British victory at Bunker Hill and the stalemate in Boston exasperated George III, who relieved Gage of his command. This portrait by John Singleton Copley shows the general in about 1768, the year he ordered British troops into Boston.

financial restitution for the tea. The alternative seemed certain ruin. Men like John Rowe—who owned one of the ships that carried the tea to Boston—had been having second thoughts about patriot tactics. Rowe offered apologies to "the Body of the People" at Old South for shipping the tea but confided to his diary that he disapproved of the Tea Party. Rowe was one of many prominent colonists who were distressed by the continued mass meetings, tarring and featherings, and other expressions of popular power. Which way would such moderates cast their loyalties?

Uncertain of merchants' support, Samuel Adams, Dr. Joseph Warren, and other popular leaders made a risky bid to mobilize rural inhabitants of the province. The Boston Committee of Correspondence bypassed the town meeting to propose a new, sweeping boycott of English trade, called the Solemn League and Covenant. Other Bostonians seized the opportunity to strike a blow against the patriots. At a town meeting, they moved to censure and abolish the Committee of Correspondence for exceeding its authority. "The better sort of people" led the effort to denounce the patriots, reported General Gage, but they were "outvoted by a great number of the lower class."

With Boston divided, patriots faced two critical challenges. First, they needed to make sure that the town would not stand isolated and starving as trade came to a standstill. Paul Revere quickly carried Boston's version of the Tea Party out of town. The Committee of Correspondence set pen to paper to rally support and the Solemn League and Covenant circulated widely for signatures. These measures rapidly bore fruit. Although many colonists disapproved of the Tea Party, they resented Parliament's drastic measures against colonial self-government and the livelihood of an entire port town.

Second, patriots had to keep alive the institutions—town meetings, newspapers, the provincial Assembly, town committees—that had sustained resistance. They would need to disobey virtually every aspect of the new laws. The Boston Committee of Correspondence consulted with the committees of neighboring towns at Faneuil Hall, under the noses of the troops. So treasonous was their project that they soon left occupied Boston for the freer air of nearby towns. The Coercive Acts, they declared, formed "a complete system of tyranny." Colonists owed no obedience to the newly-styled courts of law. Rather than cooperate with Gage's hand-picked councilors, the Assembly should meet separately as a provincial congress to govern Massachusetts. Patriots even managed to preserve their town meetings. Towns quickly convened meetings before the deadline set by law, conducted business, and then carefully adjourned—rather than dissolved—the meeting; future gatherings would be mere "continuations" of a legal meeting and not new meetings at all.

The new governor, Thomas Gage, took office in 1774. Over the summer, town after town forced his appointed council members to resign their appointments. Communities in Massachusetts and beyond enthusiastically greeted the Solemn League and Covenant. When New Yorkers waffled over the plan, patriots called for an intercolonial congress that could create a unified response to the crisis. The Massachusetts Assembly promptly chose delegates to represent them at a Continental Congress in Philadelphia.

In turn, the Congress petitioned the king, denied parliamentary authority over the colonies, and adopted a trade boycott along the lines of the Solemn League. Called the Continental Association, the boycott required each town or county to elect a "committee of inspection" to oversee the cessation of trade. Communities became widely active in boycotts again. The press filled with reports of crowds confronting importers and tea drinkers, and accounts of symbolic tea burnings, humiliations, and tarring and featherings.

So Governor Gage faced illegal revolutionary governments—continental and provincial congresses, committees, and town meetings—whose resolutions governed Massachusetts Bay far more effectively than his own. Years later, when John Adams listed the institutions that had given New England a distinctively republican character, he named the town meeting, the Congregational church, the public school, and the militia. It was the last of these that allowed patriots to maintain a "shadow government" in the face of military occupation of their capital city. The militia included all adult men, aged 16 to 60, who were required to turn out once a year to drill and

Dr. Joseph Warren, chairman of the Boston Committee of Safety and president of the Massachusetts Provincial Congress, planned the midnight rides of Paul Revere and William Dawes. He had once declared that he hoped to die fighting British "up to my knees in blood." A British officer called him "the greatest incendiary in America." Warren was in his mid-20s when John Singleton Copley painted this portrait in 1765. He was 34 years old when he was killed at Breed's Hill on June 17, 1775.

Opposite: *This unofficial list of colonial dead and wounded in the battle at Concord, April 19, 1775, was published in Boston and proved to be a very effective piece of patriot propaganda. Below it is one of the North Church lanterns that, thanks to Paul Revere, alerted patriots in Charlestown that British troops were about to leave the city.*

elect officers. In peacetime some localities had neglected this duty, but now patriots revived the militias with energy. In Concord, the Provincial Congress resolved that each town should designate one-third of its militia as "minute men," ready to turn out at the shortest notice of alarm.

In Boston, the Royal Navy had brought maritime trades to a standstill. Shipyards, ropewalks, and other ventures halted operations. Stores on the Long Wharf stood closed and shuttered. Town officials set jobless men to work at brickmaking and poor women to spinning and distributed available relief. More troops flooded into Boston. Still, newspapers continued to print diatribes against the occupation. Once again British soldiers in Boston chafed against their powerlessness. When they discovered Thomas Ditson of Billerica buying clothes and even guns in the barracks, they tarred and feathered and paraded him before the Liberty Tree.

Gage's superiors pressed the general to take decisive military action. Gage decided to act swiftly and catch the colonists by surprise, before the local militias could gather. The town of Concord offered a promising target. It was only 20 miles away, it held military stores, and the rebels' illegal Provincial Congress had just met there. Twenty-one crack companies of Regulars, a mixture of light infantry, grenadiers, and marines totaling about 700 men, prepared to march. They were commanded by Lt. Col. Francis Smith.

With solders billeted around the town, news of the British plan soon reached patriot ears. Servants and boardinghouse keepers noted unusual preparations among the troops. Paul Revere joined some 30 other men, unofficially headquartered at the Green Dragon Tavern, gathering intelligence. Patriots soon learned the destination but not the details of Gage's plan. There were two ways that the Regulars might reach the Concord road. They could march across the Neck through Roxbury or travel by boat across the Charles River to East Cambridge. Joseph Warren, in charge of the patriot camp in town, sent William Dawes, a tanner, across the Neck on horseback to alert the country people. When it became clear that the soldiers were loading into boats, Paul Revere arranged for a signal in the steeple of Old North Church: two lanterns, the prearranged sign to indicate the soldiers' route to patriots watching from across the water in Charlestown. To make doubly sure that word was out, Revere and a few associates found a boat, muffled the oars, and rowed into the darkness. At Charlestown, patriots provided the silversmith with a horse, and Revere set off toward Lexington.

By the time the British stepped out on the Concord Road, bells and cannon in the distance were rousing the country. When the redcoats neared the crossroads village of Lexington, some 70 militiamen had drawn up on the Common. For a brief moment the two forces faced each other. The militia had begun to disperse when a single shot rang out, followed by a full volley from one of the British light infantry companies. Eight militiamen were killed, 10 wounded. British officers restored order, then turned their troops toward Concord. They arrived there to find military supplies removed and a more formidable force—roughly 400 militiamen—ready to oppose them. The British set fire to the courthouse, then skirmished with the militia at the North Bridge. There were casualties on both sides. The British Regulars prudently began to retreat to Boston.

It was then that the British nightmare began. News of the fighting spread swiftly across the countryside. Through the long afternoon of April 19, militiamen converged in the thousands on the Concord to Boston road. Thomas Ditson, so recently tarred and feathered by the troops in Boston, marched with the Billerica unit. From fields and wooded groves, from behind stone walls, the provincials took aim at the scarlet coats of the retreating troops. Peppered by musket balls, the Regulars fell into disarray. Their return to Boston looked perilously like headlong flight. Not until midnight did the last of the soldiers reach the city. Casualties included 73 British and 49 colonials dead and hundreds wounded or missing. The colonies were at war, and Boston was truly under siege.

Early in May, the Second Continental Congress met at Philadelphia. Circumstances required that the delegates conduct a war even as they hoped for peace. Congress adopted New England's provisional forces as its army and placed a Virginian, George Washington, in command on June 14, 1775. They sent a last-ditch plea for reconciliation to the King.

Spring 1775: Massachusetts citizens are gathering arms and militia companies are drilling on town commons. Thomas Gage, Governor General of the colony, has twice sent British Regulars from Boston into the countryside to capture colonial military supplies, first, with success, to the Cambridge Powder House and then, unsuccessfully, to Salem, where a tense stalemate with colonials ended without bloodshed. British Lt. Frederick Mackenzie wrote, "It is certain both sides were ripe for it, and a single blow would have occasioned the commencement of hostilities." On the night of April 18, 1775, General Gage sent 700 soldiers to seize the large stockpile of military supplies in Concord, 20 miles west. The movement did not go unnoticed by the colonials, whose alarm rider network was rapidly set in motion. William Dawes, Paul Revere, and many others were soon riding westward to awaken the countryside with shouts that "the Regulars are out!" At dawn on April 19, the Regulars arrived at Lexington Common. Standing at the far end were 77 members of the Lexington Militia. It is unclear who fired first, but random shots provoked British volleys. When the smoke cleared, eight colonials lay dead and 10 were wounded—the first bloodshed of the Revolutionary War. The British troops continued on to Concord, where militia from neighboring towns were converging. As militiamen watched from a hillside, a detachment of 96 Regulars secured the North Bridge. Believing that a distant column of rising smoke meant the British were burning Concord, the colonials resolved to cross the bridge and save the town. The British soldiers fired

warning blasts, then shot directly into the advancing ranks. Maj. John Buttrick, leading the colonials, ordered his men to "Fire, for God's sake, fellow soldiers, fire!" Surprised by the colonial counter fire, the British soldiers fled. This brief fight, in which two militiamen and two Regulars were killed, signified the first time that colonials had been ordered to fire on King's troops. As the Regulars left Concord to return to Boston, gunfire broke out again and the battle escalated. For six hours the harassed Regulars had to run a gauntlet of colonial fire along the return route, known today as "Battle Road." The colonials fired from behind boulders, stone walls, trees, and houses. "We were totally surrounded by such an incessant fire as it is impossible to conceive," wrote British Ens. John Barker. (The nature of the fighting is characterized in the painting below, which is on display at the Minute Man National Historical Park Visitor Center.) By the time the exhausted British troops reached the safety of Boston Harbor, their total casualties were 73 killed and 200 wounded or missing. Colonial losses were 49 killed and 46 wounded or missing. By nightfall, nearly 20,000 colonials had mobilized. Those who arrived too late to fight on April 19 stayed to lay siege to the British in Boston and form the nucleus of the Continental Army. Years later, when asked why he risked his life to face the British troops on that fateful April morning, veteran Levi Preston replied: "We had always governed ourselves and we always meant to. They didn't mean that we should."

William Howe, considered one of the most promising young officers in the British Army, had served with distinction under the legendary Gen. James Wolfe during the French and Indian War. He had come to Boston with reinforcements and two other major generals in May 1775 to bolster Gage's besieged command. Four months after the Battle of Bunker Hill, in which his troops drove the patriots from the Charlestown Peninsula, he succeeded Gage as commander in chief.

Massachusetts faced the immediate crisis. General Gage worried that militiamen would storm the city and that most of Boston would join in an armed uprising. Gage announced that inhabitants who turned in their weapons might leave town in peace. Within weeks Bostonians of all ranks were streaming to nearby villages. In all, an estimated 12,000 to 13,000 men and women fled the city, fearing starvation, mistreatment by the British, or retaliation for their political convictions. Notorious Sons of Liberty prudently left. Benjamin Edes quietly loaded a printing press and some type into a boat, rowed to Watertown, and resumed printing the *Gazette* there. Some patriots, like John Rowe, stayed in town to oversee their property. Others, like George Robert Twelves Hewes, found themselves stuck in town when Gage decided to prevent able-bodied men from leaving after all. Those disaffected from the patriot cause, like the Cuming sisters, welcomed the protection of British troops. At the same time, Tories from the interior poured into Boston, fleeing patriot mobs and, in some cases, hoping to serve alongside the Regulars against patriot forces. The civilian population of Boston, usually about 15,000, became a mere 3,500, with an estimated two-thirds of that number being Tory sympathizers.

Surrounding the town, patriot forces hastily organized a hodgepodge of militia units from different colonies into a working army. With George Washington yet to arrive, they considered the proper chain of command and the pressing need for both ammunition and a reasonable plan of action. Massachusetts chose Artemas Ward—schoolteacher, storekeeper, provincial official, judge, and militia officer—as commander in chief of Massachusetts forces. Ward and Gage both realized that the hills surrounding Boston were the military key. Charlestown Peninsula commanded the northern end of Boston and the narrow passage into the Back Bay and Charles River. To the south lay Dorchester Peninsula. Its hills loomed over Castle Island and the entire inner harbor. A patriot entrenchment built high enough on either hill would stand out of reach of cannon aboard the warships in the harbor and could dislodge the British from Boston.

Amidst rumors of a British raid, inhabitants of Charlestown evacuated their homes in May 1775. On

June 12, Gage read a royal proclamation that declared martial law and offered pardon to rebels who now laid down their arms. Learning of a British initiative, provincial leaders resolved to hold Bunker Hill, on Charlestown Peninsula. In the early evening darkness of June 16, Col. William Prescott led 1,200 Massachusetts and Connecticut men out of Cambridge to build a redoubt—a fortified entrenchment with light artillery pieces—atop Bunker Hill. Through miscommunication or ignorance of the terrain, Prescott's men bypassed Bunker Hill and instead dug in on a smaller eminence, Breed's Hill. Patriot forces spent the night silently digging. With the first streaks of dawn, on June 17, 1775, British sailors aboard the sloop of war *Lively* spotted the entrenchment. Daylight revealed to the patriots their exposed situation. Rising above the empty streets of Charlestown, Breed's Hill was only 75 feet high. Should the British successfully bring men in from the north, they might cut off the patriots from all reinforcement or retreat. Prescott's men started a breastwork on the north side of the hill. New Hampshire militia under Col. John Stark manned a nearby rail fence that ran down the northeast slope to the Mystic River.

The British reacted swiftly. Warships in the harbor and land batteries on Copp's Hill opened fire on the redoubt, and Maj. Gen. William Howe prepared his soldiers to attack the patriot position. In the early afternoon, barges and longboats filled with scarlet-clad regulars made their way across Boston Harbor and came ashore at Moulton's Point, on the northeast corner of the peninsula where the Charlestown Navy Yard is located today. The British general made his main attack against the rail fence. As a diversion, he also ordered men to advance directly against the Breed's Hill redoubt. When snipers in Charlestown harassed the redcoats, the navy bombarded the town until it burned.

Through billows of smoke, over fences and treacherous footing, Howe's infantry marched. No sooner was the first attack turned back than the British regrouped and marched forward again in a hasty, uncoordinated assault all along the patriot front. Once again the result was a costly failure. Meanwhile, the roofs and windows of Boston filled with anxious spectators. From neighboring towns, people gathered

At the Battle of Bunker Hill, Peter Salem, a black soldier, was reported to have taken aim at Maj. John Pitcairn, the British officer who led the assault, and shot him. Later Salem was presented to Gen. George Washington as the man who killed Pitcairn. A portion of Alonzo Chappel's painting of the battle (page 62) purportedly shows Salem, although it could represent one of a number of black soldiers who took part in the fight. Peter Salem later fought in the battles of Saratoga and Stony Point.

The Battle of Bunker (or Breed's) Hill

On the afternoon of June 17, 1775, as Maj. Gen. William Howe's British troops advanced towards the defenses patriot forces had erected on the Charlestown Peninsula, legend says that Col. William Prescott told his men not to fire "until you see the whites of their eyes." This famous order, which probably was never given, has come to symbolize the determination of an inexperienced and ill-equipped colonial force confronting a highly trained army of professional British soldiers. Although popularly known as the Battle of Bunker Hill, most of the fighting actually took place on nearby Breed's Hill. Today a 221-foot granite monument marks the site of the first major battle of the American Revolution. The battle resulted from patriot efforts to thwart Lt. Gen. Thomas Gage's plans to fortify Dorchester Heights as a base from which to control entry to the port of Boston and drive the colonials from the siege lines they had erected around the town. Although they ultimately lost the battle, the colonists, under such capable leaders as William Prescott, John Stark, and Israel Putnam, repulsed two major British assaults and inflicted heavy casualties before being driven from their position. Of Howe's 2,200 ground forces and artillery engaged in the battle, nearly half (1,034) were killed or wounded. Of an estimated 2,500 to 4,000 patriots engaged, 400 to 600 were casualties, including the popu-

lar leader Dr. Joseph Warren, killed during Howe's third and final assault. A newly appointed major general, Warren had come to the battlefield wearing not a uniform but an expensive blue coat and a satin waistcoat fringed with lace. Nathanael Greene, a promising young officer from Rhode Island, wrote his brother that the colonists wished they "could Sell them another Hill at the same Price." When word of the British victory reached London, one English wit remarked: "If we have eight more such victories, there will be nobody left to bring the news." And General Gage sent a solemn warning to the secretary of state for war: "These People...are now Spirited up by a Rage and Enthusiasm, as great as ever People were possessed of, and you must proceed in earnest or give the Business up...." The image of the battle shown below left is by Alonzo Chappel, a mid-19th-century painter whose scenes of the Revolution fill many history books. He pat-terned his painting after a more famous romantic canvas by Jonathan Trumbull. Unlike Trumbull, who portrayed black patriot Peter Salem as a servant carrying his master's gun, Chappel shows him *(lower right of painting)* as a soldier on his own, priming his rifle.

Maj. John Pitcairn of the Royal Marines led the final assault on the American redoubt. He was fatally wounded by Peter Salem, one of several free blacks who fought in the battle that day.

Militiaman James Pike from Haverhill, Mass., was in the thick of the Battle of Bunker Hill. He was wounded in the British attack and his brother Simeon was killed. "I was one of the last of the Americans that retreated," he said proudly. While the drawings on his powder horn commemorate the events of April 19, 1775, his sentiments about provincials defending the symbolic Liberty Tree against British aggressors were just as valid two months later.

Portly Henry Knox, shown here late in his military career in this Gilbert Stuart portrait, was one of George Washington's most trusted officers. He was only 25 years old when the Continental Congress appointed him to organize and train Washington's Regiment of Artillery in November 1775. His epic 300-mile mission to Fort Ticonderoga to obtain what he called "a noble train of artillery" enabled Washington to successfully end the siege of Boston and force the British to evacuate. Knox remained in charge of the Continental Army artillery throughout the Revolutionary War.

around the hills to see the battle. Abigail Adams wrote to husband John: "Charlestown is laid in ashes. … How many have fallen we know not. The constant roar of the cannon is so distressing that we cannot eat, drink, or sleep."

On the scene of the fighting, Howe's troops were shaken but not defeated, and he quickly put together a third assault. This time the British stormed Breed's Hill from two sides, overrunning the breastwork and forcing their way among the defenders within the redoubt. In the last assault on the redoubt, many lost their lives—including Boston leader Dr. Joseph Warren and British Maj. John Pitcairn. The surviving patriots retreated across Charlestown Neck towards Cambridge. The British pursued only as far as Bunker Hill and there dug in. Nearly one-half of Howe's original 2,200 regulars had been killed or wounded. Patriot losses ranged between 400 and 600. The cost of the first major battle of the Revolution had been staggering to both sides.

General Gage informed his superiors of the situation: the spirit of rebellion, once thought to be limited to Boston, was rampant in the thirteen colonies. Confined to Boston and Charlestown, there was little reason for the British army to stay in the Massachusetts capital. In October, Gage was replaced by General Howe, who presided in town through a cold and difficult winter, waiting for new ships and supplies. With the new year, word reached the colonies that King George III had proclaimed his American subjects in rebellion and hired Hessian mercenaries to help subdue them.

George Washington, now in charge of the Continental Army, sent Col. Henry Knox, until recently a Boston bookseller, to Fort Ticonderoga to secure artillery pieces. Late in January, Knox's men returned with a full artillery train, the guns dragged on sledges over the winter snow. In March 1776, Washington took the initiative. Under the direction of Brig. Gen. John Thomas, American forces constructed fortifications on Dorchester Heights, just south of Boston, on the night of March 4. By daybreak, on the sixth anniversary of the Boston Massacre, a long line of earthworks and batteries overlooked the town. General Howe's first plan was to dislodge the Americans. However, the British response was thwarted by a storm and Howe decided that his position was no longer tenable: he prepared to evacuate immediately. Howe's troops barricaded the streets, plundered stores, and, in the early morning of March 17, embarked for Halifax. Roughly 1,000 Tories went with them. The American occupation of Dorchester Heights was the final act in an 11-month siege that successfully forced the British from Boston and gave Gen. George Washington his first military victory in the war.

Patriot Bostonians thankfully returned to their homes on horseback and on foot. Familiar buildings lay in ruins. British troops had used Faneuil Hall as a theater and Old South Meeting House as a riding school. They had chopped down the Liberty Tree, decimated Boston Common, used the steeple of West Church and George Hewes's shoe shop as firewood, and transformed the Brattle and Hollis street churches into barracks. There would be no easy return to normal.

Moreover, Boston and the rest of the colonies still stood a long way from liberty. The war with Britain remained to be won, independence to be claimed and then established. For all their sufferings, many colonists hesitated to renounce their allegiance to George III. Moderates worried that separation would license social disorder. The move toward independence was animated by a 47-page pamphlet whose radical ideas and irreverent tone swept through the colonies like wildfire. North and south, colonists read and talked about *Common Sense*, the work of Thomas Paine, a one-time corsetmaker from England. In biting prose, Paine attacked the principles of birth, breeding, and social superiority that upheld monarchy and aristocracy alike. "Men who look upon themselves born to reign, and others to obey, soon grow insolent," he wrote. Paine asserted the competence of ordinary people, be they mechanics or small farmers. *Common Sense* helped crystalize a decade's ferment: what had begun as defensive resistance against British tyranny was becoming a positive embrace of a new American ideal of equality.

When at last, in July of 1776, the colonies were ready to declare independence, they explained their action in language that incorporated these egalitarian ideals. The colonies were entitled to an "equal station" with other nations. The Continental Congress's premise, written by Thomas Jefferson in the Declara-

George Washington, a man of limited military experience, became commander in chief of the newly created Continental Army largely through the efforts of John Adams. Because of the need to gain full backing for the Revolution from the southern colonies, Adams supported Washington over John Hancock for the appointment. Washington had not sought the position and accepted it, he told his wife, only because to have done otherwise "would have reflected dishonour upon myself." This portrait is from Gilbert Stuart's heroic representation of Washington on Dorchester Heights just after his troops took possession of them.

Abigail Adams lived in Boston from 1768 to 1771, following closely the political activities of her husband, John, and taking part with other women in the boycott of British products and in memorial meetings for the victims of the Boston Massacre. Later she lived in Braintree on the family farm, which she managed when John was away in Philadelphia and where she saw to the education of their children. When he joked about her plea to "remember the ladies," she asked her friend, Mercy Otis Warren, to join her in "fomenting a rebellion" among the women. The portrait, a companion to the one of John Adams on page 38, was painted by Benjamin Blyth in 1766.

tion of Independence, has become justly famous, that "all Men are Created Equal." In this moment, in this founding document, some of the values that ordinary people brought to the resistance movement found expression. Though its meaning was ambiguous, the phrase linked independence to equality. It made sense to many Bostonians, who had worked their way toward this radical idea in more than a decade of struggle.

The war brought mixed fortunes for Boston's citizens. John Rowe chose the patriot side, although his decision to remain in town during the siege made his loyalties briefly suspect among some of his neighbors. He died a well-respected man in the late 1780s. George Robert Twelves Hewes took his shoemaking tools and escaped occupied Boston, then served during the war on a privateer and also in the militia. He remained a poor tradesman for the rest of his life. John Hancock and Samuel Adams each served in the Continental Congress and, later, as governor of the Commonwealth. The two Cuming sisters left for Nova Scotia with the evacuation. The early 1780s found Betsy Cuming in Halifax where she could conduct business with "not half the fatigue" as at Boston. Paul Revere served in numerous ways during the Revolution, including as lieutenant colonel in the Massachusetts Artillery. After the war, he expanded his business in a new shop in the North End. He opened an iron foundry where he cast church bells. His copper manufactory later produced the sheet that covered the top of the New State House on Beacon Hill and the bottom of the frigate *Constitution*. Benjamin Edes had the honor of leading the contingent of Boston printers that marched in the Grand Procession to celebrate the Constitution in 1788. Over the next decade, the *Gazette's* circulation dwindled rapidly. Edes's last years were spent in financial decline.

On the broader canvas of American society, the impulse toward social levelling moved far beyond what most patriots had foreseen. John Adams wrote in the year of independence: "We have been told that our Struggle has loosened the bands of Government every where. That Children and Apprentices were disobedient—that schools and Colledges were grown turbulent—that Indians slighted their Guardians and Negroes grew insolent to their Masters." Conservative fears were justified: men of property and learning could not fully control the changes taking place in American institutions. Patriots had begun with a deep commitment to British liberty—including the idea that even those of little property and standing ought to be able to make their notions of right and justice felt. In the course of resistance, there arose the idea that the people's will provided the very basis of all authority.

The egalitarian impulse would reach deeply into the lives of many. John Adams's remark had been in reply to his wife, Abigail, who had boldly suggested that patriot principles should affect the very relationship of marriage: "In the new Code of Laws which I suppose it will be necessary for you to make I desire you would Remember the Ladies, and be more generous and favourable to them than your ancestors. Do not put such unlimited power into the hands of husbands. Remember, all Men would be tyrants if they could." Congress in fact did nothing to change the legal rights of wives. Yet the war brought a host of new experiences for women. Their pre-war resistance activities had introduced many to the idea that they were political beings, capable of judging government acts and choosing an allegiance. With warfare women shouldered new responsibilities. In the absence of their menfolk, they ran farms and businesses, raised children, and made household decisions in difficult and unpredictable times. After the war, conservative ideas sharply limited women's political gains. But with increasing success women claimed the need for their own education and asserted the importance of their role as wives and mothers in shaping citizens of the republic. In 1789, Boston opened its public schools to girls.

Similarly, sentiment against the slave trade and slavery itself grew more pronounced throughout New England. African Americans not-so-humbly petitioned for liberation from a state "worse than Nonexistence." Prompted by such slave petitions, the Massachusetts legislature considered a bill to end slavery. But it was the courts that ended slavery in the Bay state. The state's new constitution, adopted in 1780, included the phrase "all men are born free and equal." When runaway slave Quok Walker was sued by his master, his defense rested on those words. In 1783, the Masschusetts Supreme Court ruled that

The Fortification of Dorchester Heights

By the late autumn of 1775, Gen. George Washington faced a serious military dilemma. He knew the British could expect supplies to arrive in the spring and he saw apathy beginning to grow among his men, but he lacked powder and artillery to rout the besieged British from their stronghold in Boston. Dorchester Heights, a high point of pastureland reaching into Boston Harbor, had drawn the general's attention as early as August. In November, he sent Col. Henry Knox to Fort Ticonderoga in New York to retrieve captured British artillery and powder. Knox's mission proved successful in February 1776 and Washington could finally act. By occupying Dorchester Heights, Washington hoped to draw the British out of Boston. On the night of March 4, colonial soldiers, led by John Thomas, hastily fortified the frozen heights. The British commander, Maj. Gen. William Howe, attempted a full-scale attack on the position the following day, but a storm prevented him from reaching it. With the colonials now well-entrenched and threatening further action, Howe prepared to leave the city for Nova Scotia, taking with him many loyalists. On March 17, 1776, the British abandoned Boston, giving Washington his first major victory of the war.

The abolitionist era in the North preceding the Civil War provided a major impetus for the rediscovery of African-American heroes of the Revolutionary era. Boston's antislavery leaders made constant analogies between their fight to end slavery and the ideals of freedom embodied in the struggle for independence. In the speeches of abolitionists, antislavery activists were likened to the Sons of Liberty. William Cooper Nell, an African-American abolitionist and historian, wrote a groundbreaking study in 1855, *The Colored Patriots of the American Revolution.* Abolitionists could also point to the triumph of the slave Phillis Wheatley, a member of the congregation at Old South Meeting House, who in 1773 was the first African American to publish a book of poetry. She stood as a shining example to prove that blacks were not intellectually inferior beings. Crispus Attucks, an escaped slave and the first colonist to die in the Boston Massacre, later became a powerful symbol of the quest for freedom for many abolitionists. In the Battle of Bunker Hill, sharpshooters like Peter Salem picked off a number of British officers. Salem, together with Barzillai Lew, Salem Prince, and other black patriots, fought valiantly in this legendary engagement. African Americans

This silk flag bearing the initials JGWH, a pine tree, a deer, and a scroll containing the unit's name was presented by John Hancock to the Bucks of America, Boston's little-known all-black military company of the Revolution. Right: Phillis Wheatley was the first black, the first slave, and the third woman in America to publish a book of poems. Far right: This "humble Petition of many Slaves" to Gov. Thomas Hutchinson and the Massachusetts General Court in January 1773 was the first public protest against slavery made by blacks to a legislature in New England.

Province of the MASSACHUSETTS-BAY.

To his Excellency
THOMAS HUTCHINSON, Esq;
GOVERNOR ;
To the Honorable
His Majesty's COUNCIL, and

To the Honorable House of REPRESENTATIVES in General Court assembled at BOSTON, the 6th Day of *January*, 1773.

The humble PETITION of many SLAVES, living in the Town of BOSTON, and other Towns in the Province is this, namely, viewed the Revolutionary War as an opportunity to free themselves from slavery, whether as patriot, loyalist, runaway, or neutral. In the wake of the ideals and rhetoric unleashed by the Revolution, it was difficult for Massachusetts to sustain the institution of slavery, which was formally abolished in the state in 1783. A vibrant free black community developed on Boston's Beacon Hill, constructing the African Meeting House in 1806, one of the oldest extant black churches in the United States. The end of slavery did not mean the end of racial prejudice. The struggle to integrate Boston's schools in part played out in the Abiel Smith School, which, along with the African Meeting House and the Black Heritage Trail, is managed by the Boston African American National Historic Site and the Museum of Afro American History. They afford glimpses into the world of the free black community of 19th-century Boston. A hotbed of abolitionism, this community celebrated its Revolutionary-era ancestors as role models and trailblazers while they fought to end slavery throughout the United States and fulfill the unkept promise of the American Revolution.

William C. Nell, black historian and abolitionist, led the campaign that ended school segregation in Boston in 1855. Left: *Built in 1806, the African Meeting House is the oldest black church building still standing in the United States. William Lloyd Garrison founded the New England Anti-Slavery Society here in 1832. In 1863, the 54th Massachusetts Infantry, made up of free black volunteers, used the building as a recruiting center. The meeting house is sometimes called "the Black Faneuil Hall."*

the words of the constitution meant what they said. Elsewhere, too, African Americans struggled for liberty. Some fought on the patriot side, but others sought freedom on the British side. After the war, the desires of white Americans for intercolonial union blunted their antislavery fervor. The U.S. Constitution secured an alliance with southern states in part by protecting slavery and the slave trade. Not until 1865, with the ratification of the 13th amendment to the Constitution, was slavery finally abolished in the United States.

For ordinary free men, such as small farmers and tradesmen, the Revolution brought a new mode of activity, a new political identity to replace that of the colonial era. In the course of the resistance, men of little property had claimed the right to be consulted. In increasing numbers, farmers and mechanics had come to participate not just in crowds but on revolutionary committees, in newspaper debates, and at public meetings. Through the long years of warfare, the men who served in Washington's army and in non-combat roles became more assertive of such rights. They claimed the right to organize, to vote, to publish their sentiments, and to take part in the politics of state and nation. In the 1780s, such voters shocked conservatives by electing men of humble background to the state legislatures. Conservatives drafted the U.S. Constitution, which moved power from the states, where ordinary voters had influence, to the federal level, where they would have less. Yet even a conservative Constitutional Convention knew they could not hope to gain approval for their frame of government if they deviated too greatly from "the genius of the people."

Over the decades, Bostonians continued to show what the Revolution meant to them. In the 1780s and 1790s, writer Judith Sargent Murray challenged "the idea of the incapability of women" and argued that serious education would help women gain their own independence. At the same time, free black Bostonians established collective institutions—a Masonic Lodge, an African Meeting House and a school. Led by Prince Hall, they petitioned, organized, and agitated on behalf of the revolutionary ideal of equal rights. Generations of working people—the so-called "lower orders"—remained inspired by the Revolution. In 1832, Bostonian Seth Luther argued that "we the people" meant not just wealthy manufacturers, but the many who labored 12 hours a day in the region's cotton mills. Claiming workers' right to organize to improve conditions, Luther reminded listeners that there were precedents for popular organization: the people had once collectively combined to use "Boston harbour as a tea pot." For such Bostonians as these, the Revolution remained vital and in some respects unfinished.

In the long run, indeed, Boston's resistance and America's revolution produced new debates and new questions about liberty on into the 19th and 20th centuries. The claim that all should have a voice, the goal of equality—these ideas brought continuing struggles over politics, economy, and culture. In a sense, the legacy of the Revolution lay in the struggle itself, in the open-ended nature of its concept of liberty. In Boston, such sites as Faneuil Hall, the Old State House, Bunker Hill Monument, the Dorchester Heights Monument, the Paul Revere House, Old North Church, the African Meeting House, and Old South Meeting House stand to remind us that the implications of American liberty still face those who walk Boston's streets today.

Part 2

Travels in Historic Boston

One of the special charms of Boston has always been its wealth of vibrant and active historic sites, especially those related to the American Revolutionary period. While a handful of other U.S. cities can trace their origins as far back as Boston, most have bulldozed and built over their historic structures, or lost the original buildings to fire and other misfortunes.

Not so in Boston. Starting in the 1870s, partly in anticipation and appreciation of the 1876 United States Centennial, Bostonians began saving a variety of buildings linked to America's colorful and rebellious past. A century later, in 1974, Congress and the National Park Service ensured the continuity of this effort—and the preservation of important parts of America's heritage—by creating Boston National Historical Park. The park has proved vital in helping to link, interpret, and preserve nationally prominent historic places throughout Boston.

Today, Boston National Historical Park is an association of sites ranging from steepled churches, Revolutionary-period graveyards, and grand meeting halls to quaint colonial homes, shops, battlegrounds, and America's oldest commissioned warship. With its elements scattered throughout the city, the park is unique, mixing historic buildings and landscapes owned by the city, the state, the federal government, and a variety of private organizations.

Visitors can start their journey into the Revolutionary era by picking up information at Boston National Historical Park visitor centers at 15 State Street or the Charlestown Navy Yard, and at the Greater Boston Convention and Visitors Bureau Center on Boston Common and in the Prudential Center. National Park Service ranger-guided programs are also available.

Since Boston is the consummate walking city, the best way to explore the park is by meandering all or part of the 2.5-mile **Freedom Trail**,® which links 16 of these sites: Boston Common, the Massachusetts State House, Park Street Church, the Granary Burying Ground, King's Chapel, King's Chapel Burying Ground, the site of America's first public school, Old South Meeting House, the Old Corner Bookstore, the Old State House, the Boston Massacre Site, Faneuil Hall, the Paul Revere House, Old North Church, Copp's Hill Burying Ground, the Bunker Hill Monument, and U.S.S *Constitution* in the historic Charlestown Navy Yard. A red line of inlaid brick and overlaid paint will guide you along the route.

Two miles south of downtown Boston is the hillside where the Continental Army under the leadership of Gen. George Washington set its cannon and forced the British evacuation of Boston on March 17, 1776. A colonial revival-style marble tower now marks **Dorchester Heights**, commemorating this first, and bloodless, victory for the Continental Army and its new commander. Each year Bostonians still celebrate March 17 as Evacuation Day— which conveniently coincides with the ever-popular St. Patrick's Day.

Boston's African-American population played a role in the Revolutionary era. Names like Phillis Wheatley, Crispus Attucks, and Peter Salem were inextricably intertwined with the city's literary, radical-political, and military history of the period. Moreover, the cries of freedom and equality echoing from the war years did not go unheard. By 1783, slavery had been declared unconstitutional in the Commonwealth of Massachusetts.

But freedom, it was soon discovered,

had little to do with equality. Hence, the 19th century became a time of struggle for another kind of independence, as Boston's African Americans and their allies fought to establish equal education, end American slavery, and create independent supportive institutions by and for blacks.

In 1980, six years after it had created Boston National Historical Park, Congress enacted legislation establishing the **Boston African American National Historic Site** on Beacon Hill. Like Boston National Historical Park, this newer National Park Service unit includes many extant structures, both public and private, some of which have since been restored with the aid of federal funding. The site's keystone structure is the 1806 African Meeting House, constructed by free black and white artisans. There is also a spectacular public memorial to Robert Gould Shaw and the 54th Massachusetts Regiment. Created by Augustus Saint-Gaudens and located opposite the Massachusetts State House, the monument is a tribute to the Union Army's first all-black volunteer Civil War regiment organized in the North.

The walking tour for the Boston African American National Historic Site—in essence, a counterpart to the Freedom Trail—is the **Black Heritage Trail.** This trail, which began during the 1960s Civil Rights era, consists of a 1.6-mile self- or ranger-guided walk through the quiet, quaint, tree-lined streets of Beacon Hill. Tales of runaway slaves, the Underground Railroad, abolitionist orators, African Americans in the Union army, and fights to desegregate Boston's schools in the 1840s are just part of the history embodied in the 14-site trek.

Tours of the African Meeting House, Abiel Smith School, and the Black Heritage Trail, as well as exhibits and special programs, are offered through the Museum of Afro American History and Boston African American National Historic Site.

Robert Gould Shaw/54th Massachusetts Regiment Memorial by Augustus Saint-Gaudens

MONUMENT
SQUARE
High St

**Bunker Hill
Monument**

Chelsea St
**Forge
Shop**

Ropewalk

Gate 4
1st Ave
5th St

Boston Marine Society

Monument
Square

Adams St

TRAINING
FIELD

Winthrop St

Main St

Chelsea St

**Commandant's
House**

**USS Constitution
Museum**

Building 5

SHIPYARD
PARK
**Massachusetts
Korean War
Veterans Memorial**

• Water Shuttle Dock

CHARLESTOWN

CITY
SQUARE
PARK

Constitution Rd

Gate

**U.S.S.
Constitution**

**CHARLESTOWN NAVY
YARD**

**U.S.S.
Cassin Young**

Rutherford Ave

Visitor Center

National Park
Service boundary

93

FREEDOM TRAIL

**PAUL
REVERE
PARK**

Charlestown Bridge

North Washington St

CHARLES RIVER

Water shuttle
to Long Wharf

BOSTON INNER HARBOR

**Museum
of Science
Hayden Planetarium**

JOHN F. FITZGERALD EXPRESSWAY

Commercial St

**Copp's Hill
Burying
Ground**

Hull St

**Old North
Church**

PAUL REVERE
MALL

**St. Stephen's
Church**

Causeway

Washington St

NORTH END

**Paul
Revere
House**

Prince St

Charles St

APPROXIMATE 1775 SHORELINE

**Pierce-Hichborn
House**

Hanover St

Cross St

North St

Richmond St

**NORTH
SQUARE**

**Harrison Gray
Otis House**

**Old West
Church**

Cambridge

**BLACK HERITAGE
TRAIL**

**Lewis and
Harriet
Hayden
House**

**John Coburn
House**

Irving St

Joy St

**Smith Court
Residences**

Congress St

Hanover St

Marshall St

Union St

Holocaust Memorial

North Market

▲ Phillips St

**African Meeting
House**

**Abiel Smith
School**

Faneuil Hall

Quincy Market

South Market

State St

LONG WHARF

Water
Shuttle
Dock

BEACON HILL

Phillips School

Pinckney St

**Massachusetts
State House**

**Old State
House**

**Boston
Massacre Site**

**Custom
House**

**New England
Aquarium**

**John J.
Smith
House**

Cedar Lane Way

W. Cedar St

**George
Middleton
House**

Joy St

**King's Chapel
and Burying
Ground**

Court St

**Benjamin
Franklin
Statue**

**Visitor
Center**

93

**Charles
Street
Meeting
House**

**Nichols
House**

**Boston
Athenaeum**

School St

**First
Public
School
Site**

**Old Corner
Bookstore**

**Prescott
House**

**Robert Gould Shaw/54th
Massachusetts
Regiment Memorial**

**Granary
Burying
Ground**

**Old South
Meeting
House**

Beacon St

Frog Pond

Tremont St

Park St

**Park
Street
Church**

Washington St

Congress St

**Visitor
Information**

**Boston
Common**

Summer St

Atlantic Ave

**Boston
Tea Party
marker**

PUBLIC GARDEN

Charles St

**Central
Burying
Ground**

Essex St

Boylston St

FORT POINT CHANNEL

0   0.1 Kilometer 0.3
0   0.1 Mile   0.3

Ⓣ Rapid Transit stop

Approximate land area in 1775

In some ways, the Freedom Trail is as old as Boston itself. The Common was set aside as a public park as early as 1634, only four years after the town was founded. A year later Boston opened its first public school. By 1661 the town boasted three urban burial grounds, followed by countless churches, meetinghouses, homes, and public buildings. Though many disappeared with time and in a multitude of "great fires," others survived to play a role in the American Revolution.

While the sites were there for centuries, it wasn't until 1951 that Bob Winn, a member of the Old North Church, and *Boston Herald-Traveler* journalist Bill Schofield offered a revolutionary twist to these landmarks. Schofield wrote a series of editorials arguing that Boston had an unusual concentration of historic sites related to our nation's turbulent beginnings, but that tourists could generally find only two or three of them. Since so many of these landmarks were located within easy walking distance of one another, Schofield challenged the city to "connect the dots" with a walking tour.

By June 1951, an early incarnation of Boston's Freedom Trail had been born. Over the next two decades, the trail grew in popularity and prestige, soon becoming an international tourist destination. Many of the individual sites on the trail had developed their own personalities and programs, offering visitors exhibits, interpretation, gift shops, activities, and even the occasional costumed historic character. In 1974, a wide variety of groups who had nurtured and financed the trail for years were joined by the National Park Service, when Boston National Historical Park was created.

Today, ranger programs are available at various National Park Service sites.

Visitors can also take self-guided tours, after picking up guidemaps, pamphlets, and books at 15 State Street, the Greater Boston Convention and Visitors Bureau Center on Boston Common, the Boston National Historical Park Visitor Center at Charlestown Navy Yard, or the seasonal visitor contact station at the Bunker Hill Monument. Visitors are encouraged to use public transportation and walk, rather than drive in downtown Boston. A wide variety of tours, exhibits, lectures, educational programs, and special events are offered by the National Park Service and along the Freedom Trail at its varied sites. Information about these activities is available at Boston National Historical Park Visitor Center, phone 617-242-5642, or the Charlestown Navy Yard Visitor Center at 617-242-5601. You may also write to the Superintendent, Boston National Historical Park, Charlestown Navy Yard, Boston, MA 02129. The park's Internet address is www.nps.gov/bost.

Though some visitors choose to trek the entire 2.5-mile route or select an individual site to visit at length, others experience the Freedom Trail through its four "chapters," organized along geographic and thematic lines. In Chapter I, *Revolution of Minds and Hearts*, visitors travel through tales of colonial days and ways from Boston Common to King's Chapel Burying Ground. In Chapter II, *The People Revolt*, they move from Old South Meeting House to Faneuil Hall and learn how independent-minded Bostonians began to protest and resist British rule. Chapter III focuses on the North End, the home of Paul Revere and the *Neighborhood of Revolution*. The final chapter, *Boston Goes to War*, focuses on Charlestown and features historic battlefields and famous naval vessels.

For more than a century before the first musket was fired in America's War for Independence, Puritan-bred Bostonians embraced a strong heritage of community and a culture of freedom that was remarkable among colonial settlements. The sites here include places where townsfolk assembled to proclaim their rights, drill their militia, bury their dead, educate their young, govern their own church congregations, and protect their lands from British meddling. "The Revolution was effected before the war commenced," observed John Adams. "The Revolution was in the minds and hearts of the people...."

Boston Common In 1634, four years after they founded the town of Boston, the Puritans of the Massachusetts Bay Colony bought a 48-acre tract of land on the slopes of Beacon Hill as an English-style "commonage," or common area, for the use of all Boston's residents. Though today we view the Common as a tree-lined park filled with rambling walkways, memorial statues, vendors, concerts, ballgames, street performers, a visitor center, city or ranger-guided tours, the Frog Pond, and the Park Street subway stop, its uses were far different in colonial times.

In the 17th and 18th centuries, the land here was sparsely planted, with a great elm as its most prominent feature. While sledding, promenading, and ball playing were part of colonial life, Bostonians also used the Common as a military training field, cow and sheep pasture, public execution site, and burial ground. Patriots often met here, exercising their rights of assembly and free speech. Prior to the War for Independence, British regulars camped and drilled here as well.

Massachusetts State House While Boston and the colonies lived under British rule, the seat of government was in the building we now call the Old State House. Following the Revolution, Bostonians and other citizens of the Massachusetts Commonwealth envisioned a grander structure, representing their new prosperity and political independence.

Since 1798, the elegant *new* State House—a neoclassical/Federal style structure originally designed by Boston's own Charles Bulfinch—has been home to the governor, State Senate, and House of Representatives of the Commonwealth. Filled with unique sculptures, stained glass, mosaics, paintings, and decorative marble, and echoing with colorful historical anecdotes, the State House is also the center of everyday Massachusetts political activity. The front of the State House faces the famed Shaw/54th Massachusetts Regiment memorial on Boston Common, and is easily recognized by its golden dome. Once clad in copper by the enterprising Paul Revere, the dome is the center of Boston for mapmaking purposes: if a sign reads, "Boston—6 miles," that indicates the distance to the gilded dome.

Park Street Church and Granary Burying Ground These two sites lie just down the hill from the State House. Though located adjacent to one another, they are unrelated. Urban legend suggests that the Georgian-style brick Congregational Church was called

Boston Common and the Public Garden dominate this aerial view of downtown Boston. The Massachusetts State House (upper left) *sits near the apex of the triangle and the beginning of the Freedom Trail.*

"Brimstone Corner," either because of the gunpowder stored here in the War of 1812 or the hellfire-and-brimstone sermons given here in the 1820s and 1830s. Still an active community church, the Park Street Church hosted William Lloyd Garrison's first antislavery speech. Granary Burying Ground, founded in 1660, contains more than 2,000 gravestones and tombs. Its permanent residents include prestigious patriots like Paul and Sarah Revere, John Hancock, and Samuel Adams, as well as the Boston Massacre victims and a woman popularly known as "Mother Goose."

King's Chapel and Burying Ground
When Boston's Puritans refused to sell land for the building of an Anglican Church, the British royal governor, Sir Edmund Andros, seized a parcel from the town's oldest cemetery and built the first King's Chapel in 1688. (The present structure was built in 1754.) After the Revolution, the congregation converted King's Chapel into America's first Unitarian Church, which remains active today. Those buried in the old Puritan graveyard next door include outspoken colonials like John Winthrop, *Mayflower* traveller Mary Chilton, patriot rider William Dawes, and a woman some believe inspired Nathaniel Hawthorne's *The Scarlet Letter.*

First Public School   The site of this colonial precursor to the famous Boston Latin School is marked by a folk-art mosaic on the sidewalk behind King's Chapel. The school was established in 1635 and the first schoolhouse was built here in 1645. A bronze statue of Benjamin Franklin, who attended the school for a brief time, stands nearby.

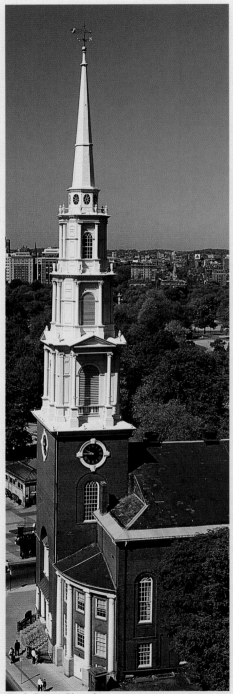

Park Street Church

Granary Burying Ground

Headstone, King's Chapel Burying Ground

In the year 1760, virtually no Bostonians even considered breaking away from Great Britain. Between 1761 and 1775, however, differing views of the rights of the colonies under British rule led to actions, reactions, and tumultuous encounters between Britain and the Boston colonists that snowballed toward war. The sites here feature places where liberty-loving men and women began to take collective action, culminating in events like the Boston Tea Party.

Old South Meeting House For colonial Bostonians, a "meeting house" was both a religious and community center, where citizens assembled to worship, voice opinions, and host celebrations, rallies, protests, and other events. Before Faneuil Hall was enlarged to its present size in 1805, the Old South Meeting House, built in 1729, was Boston's biggest building and *the* meeting hall for large events.

Patriots Samuel Adams and Joseph Warren were among those who mesmerized crowds here, stoking the flames of rebellion with meetings like the annual vigil for the victims of the Boston Massacre. On the night of December 16, 1773, some 5,000 patriots crammed into the hall to protest the British tax on tea. With his carefully-worded secret signal—"This meeting can do nothing more to save the country"—Adams invited the crowd to descend on Griffin's Wharf for the infamous Boston Tea Party. British troops later avenged this indignity by turning Old South into a riding school and filling it with horses.

Throughout its history, Old South has boasted many illustrious firsts. Slave-poet Phillis Wheatley, the first African American to publish a book of poems, was a congregation member.

Ben Franklin was baptized here. In the 1870s, Old South was saved first from the Great Fire of 1872 and then, a few years later, from the wrecking ball, becoming New England's first successful preservation effort. No longer a church, Old South remains an icon of free speech and assembly, and a center for educational activities.

Old Corner Bookstore Constructed as an apothecary and private residence, and set on the original homesite of freethinker Anne Hutchinson, the Old Corner building is one of central Boston's few surviving examples of early 18th-century domestic architecture. It gained international renown in the mid-l9th century as Ticknor & Fields' publishing house and bookstore, a mecca for American and British literati. Saved in the 1960s when civic leaders founded Historic Boston Incorporated, the building now houses retail and office tenants.

Old State House Built in 1713, Boston's oldest surviving public building has served the city in a variety of capacities, including as merchants' exchange, state house, city hall, court house, post office, and even wine cellar. British governors who held forth here in colonial times, when it was known as the Towne House, were promptly replaced by locally elected officials in the wake of the American Revolution. In 1761, patriot James Otis eloquently argued here against the British Writs of Assistance. "Then and there...," recalled John Adams years later, "the child Independence was born."

On July 18, 1776, the second floor balcony was the site from which the Declaration of Independence was first read to Bostonians. Later that evening, carved figures of the royal lion and

Old South Meeting House

Old State House

Old Corner Bookstore

unicorn were angrily torn from the roof. Today, replicas of those figures once again adorn the Old State House roof, serving as reminders of pre-revolutionary days.

Though the landmark was threatened with demolition in the 1870s, it was saved and preserved by a group that became The Bostonian Society. That active group still operates the beautifully ornate building and its vibrant museum of Boston history.

Boston Massacre Site   Right below the Old State House balcony is a small circle of stones surrounded by a traffic island. Though unobtrusive and often unnoticed, the site commemorates an incident remembered as the Boston Massacre. On March 5, 1770, a street scuffle erupted between Bostonians and British soldiers. Hurled snowballs, rocks, and insults led to a frantic round of British musket fire, leaving five colonials dead—and destined for martyrdom. The site remains a popular stop for tour groups and annual reenactments.

Faneuil Hall   With its gilded grasshopper weathervane and red-brick Georgian exterior, historic Faneuil Hall looks as pristinely elegant as any "Cradle of Liberty" should. Once a food market and now a retail space, the ground floor level offers visitors a place to browse and shop. Guests can also frequent a variety of events—from historic tours, political rallies, and concerts, to receptions, solemn ceremonies, and debates—in the columned, neoclassical Great Hall above.

It was on the second floor of the original building that patriots often rallied and railed against British oppression. Beginning in 1763, patriot Sam Adams and his colleagues ushered in the greatest period of town meetings in Boston history in this hall. Sculptor Anne Whitney's statue of Adams stands guard behind the building. Illustrious speakers here have included Susan B. Anthony, Frederick Douglass, and John F. Kennedy.

Completed in 1742, Faneuil Hall was rebuilt after it burned down in 1761. In 1805-06, Boston had the hall's size doubled to its present proportions, hiring celebrated architect Charles Bulfinch to oversee the project.

The top floor of Faneuil Hall is the long-time home of the Ancient and Honorable Artillery Company, which has occupied the building since 1746. The Hall faces bustling Quincy Market, the 19th-century marketplace renovated into a modern shoppers' and food-lovers' paradise.

An ancient and honorable crest. Right: *The Great Hall on Faneuil Hall's second floor hosted many revolutionary gatherings.*

In the course of just two pivotal days—April 18 and 19, 1775—years of growing unrest burst into insurrection. Among the families living in the North End, Boston's oldest surviving residential neighborhood, were middle class artisan Paul Revere, his second wife Rachel, and seven of his children. It was patriot Revere who planned the hanging of warning lanterns in the steeple of the Old North Church on April 18. By morning, colonial militia had assembled in Lexington and Concord, for what became the first military encounters of the Revolution.

Paul Revere House   With its painted clapboard siding, diamond-shaped window panes, and dark roof overhang, the building at 19 North Square looks like a vestige of medieval times. It's not quite *that* old, but the Paul Revere House is the oldest house in downtown Boston, the only home on the Freedom Trail, and an historic centerpiece of the engagingly old world North End. When silversmith Revere bought the home in 1770, it was already close to a century old. The neighborhood was a curious mix, ranging from middle-class artisans and wealthy Tories to seafaring fellows and African-American families. The period furniture inside today reflects both Revere's era and that of Robert Howard, the home's first owner.

On the night of April 18, 1775, Revere left his home and wife Rachel to begin his famous "Midnight Ride," warning patriots in the countryside of the British approach. Henry Wadsworth Longfellow's legendary 1861 poem, "Paul Revere's Ride," helped make both Revere and Longfellow household names. Though that poem is inaccurate at best, it provided international fame for the story of the ride.

Meanwhile, visitors to the Revere House soon find that many lesser-known tales from this building are equally interesting. In the 19th century, the house—and the adjacent Pierce-Hichborn House, belonging to Revere's cousin—were both crowded tenements, serving the influx of immigrants whose first stop was often the North End. The house was renovated and restored in 1906-08 by the Paul Revere Memorial Association, a landmark event in preservation history.

Old North Church   The two lanterns that warned colonists in Charlestown that British regulars were approaching "by sea"—across the Charles River—were hung by sexton Robert Newman from the steeple of the venerable Old North on April 18, 1775. Officially named the Christ Church in Boston, the Old North (built in 1723) is Boston's oldest church building and remains an active Episcopal church. Beautiful artwork, gardens, box pews, and a Georgian-style brick exterior augment its association with the dramatic exploits of Paul Revere and his colleagues.

Copp's Hill Burying Ground   Established in 1660, Copp's Hill is Boston's second oldest burying ground, and the final resting place of numerous colonial-era free African Americans, artisans, craftspersons, and merchants. Lantern-hanger Robert Newman is interred here, as is the black activist Prince Hall and Puritan minister Cotton Mather. British soldiers camped here in 1775 fired shells onto Charlestown during the Battle of Bunker Hill.

Paul Revere House

Copp's Hill Burying Ground

Old North Church interior

Less than two months after Lexington and Concord, patriots endured one of the bloodiest encounters of the War for Independence—the Battle of Bunker Hill. Though the British won the battle, their losses were immense, inspiring patriots to continue armed resistance. By 1783, the United States had won its independence. The seemingly invincible U.S.S. *Constitution* was one of the frigates the newly-formed U.S. Navy built to defend the young nation against pirates, the British, or any other would-be challengers.

Bunker Hill Monument In April 1775, patriots defended themselves in fighting at Lexington and Concord. Two months later, on June 17, colonial and British forces clashed on Charlestown's Breed's Hill in a brutal confrontation that left more than 500 patriots and 1,000 British regulars dead or wounded. Though the British took the hill, the misnamed "Battle of Bunker Hill" demonstrated patriot ability to resist well-trained "redcoats" and led the colonies to form their own army, thus launching the Revolutionary War in earnest.

Fifty years after the battle, Bostonians decided to commemorate this event with a 221-foot Egyptian obelisk. When funds for completing the monument ran out, a spectacular weeklong women-run "Fair"—essentially a grand bake and crafts sale—saved the day. At the base of the monument stands a heroic statue of Col. William Prescott, and a ground-level lodge features exhibits on the battle. The top of the monument, a climb of 294 steps, offers a stellar view of the city.

U.S.S. *Constitution* Nicknamed "Old Ironsides" for the way enemy cannonballs bounced off its sturdy wooden hull, U.S.S. *Constitution* was built in nearby Hartt's shipyard and launched in 1797 as part of America's first naval fleet. *Constitution* battled Barbary corsairs in the Mediterranean and British warships in the War of 1812. Periodic efforts to scrap the old vessel over the decades were always met by public resistance and massive fundraising campaigns to "Save Our Ship." Touring the ship is a must, as is visiting the nearby **USS Constitution Museum**, which offers state-of-the-art displays, exhibits, artifacts, ship models, activities, and shows.

U.S.S. *Constitution* is the acknowledged centerpiece of the beautifully renovated **Charlestown Navy Yard**, heralded as one of the first naval yards in America. It was commissioned in 1800 to build, maintain, and supply ships for the U.S. Navy. Until its decommissioning in 1974, this was a bustling site filled with dry docks, ropewalks, sailors, and shipways. During World War II, some 50,000 men and women—including Boston's own "Rosie the Riveters"— built, repaired, and supplied ships here. One of the ships refitted in the yard in the 1950s was the **U.S.S. *Cassin Young***, which is maintained today as a popular visitation site. An illustrated National Park Service handbook recounting the history of the navy yard is available at park visitor centers.

Bunker Hill Monument and Prescott statue   *U.S.S.* Constitution

Charlestown Navy Yard and U.S.S. Cassin Young

Minute Man National Historical Park in Concord, Lincoln, and Lexington preserves the scene of the fighting between colonists and British troops on April 19, 1775. The North Bridge *(right)* is the site of the "shot heard 'round the world." Historic sites in the Battle Road area of the park are connected by the Battle Road Trail. This pathway for walking, bicycle, or wheelchair follows remnants of the original road and includes historic houses, fields, wetlands, and forests. The park visitor center features an audiovisual program, exhibits, and a bookstore.

Adams National Historic Site in Quincy includes the birthplaces of the second and sixth United States Presidents, John Adams and his son, John Quincy Adams. Abigail Adams, an eminent patriot and a very significant figure in American history, was a true partner and equal to her husband John. She and John Quincy viewed the Battle of Bunker Hill from Penn's Hill, part of the family farm, and the experience had a profound effect on both of them. At this site, John Adams, Samuel Adams, and James Bowdoin drafted the Massachusetts Constitution.

Longfellow National Historic Site in Cambridge is the home of Henry Wadsworth Longfellow, the first nationally famous American poet. Longfellow and his wife Fanny felt great pride that their house had served as Gen. George Washington's headquarters from July 15, 1775, to April 2, 1776. During that time, Washington formed the Continental Army and fortified Dorchester Heights. This latter action led to Washington's first military victory—the British evacuation of Boston on March 17, 1776. Longfellow lived here from 1837 to 1882.

Bailyn, Bernard, *The Ordeal of Thomas Hutchinson.* Harvard University Press, 1974.

Berlin, Ira, and Ronald Hoffman, editors, *Slavery and Freedom in the Age of the American Revolution.* University of Illinois Press, 1986.

Bober, Natalie, *Abigail Adams: Witness to a Revolution.* Atheneum Books for Young Readers, 1995.

Bobrick, Benson, *Angel in the Whirlwind: The Triumph of the American Revolution.* Simon & Schuster, 1997.

Commager, Henry S., and Richard B. Morris, editors, *The Spirit of Seventy-Six: The Story of the American Revolution As Told by Participants.* Harper & Row, 1967.

Countryman, Edward, *The American Revolution.* Hill & Wang, 1985.

DePauw, Linda Grant, *Founding Mothers: Women of America in the Revolutionary Era.* Houghton Mifflin, 1975.

Dunwell, Steve, and Blanche M. G. Linden, *Boston Freedom Trail.* Back Bay Press, 1996.

Fischer, David Hackett, *Paul Revere's Ride.* Oxford University Press, 1994.

Forbes, Esther, *Paul Revere and the World He Lived In.* Houghton Mifflin, 1942.

Fowler, William M., *Samuel Adams: Radical Puritan.* Longman, 1997.

Galvin, John R., *The Minute Men: A Compact History of the Defenders of the American Colonies, 1645-1775.* Hawthorn Books, 1967.

Hoffman, Ronald, and Peter J. Albert, editors, *The Transforming Hand of Revolution: Reconsidering the American Revolution as a Social Movement.* University Press of Virginia, 1996.

Kaplan, Sidney, and Emma Nogrady Kaplan, *The Black Presence in the Era of the American Revolution.* University of Massachusetts Press, 1989.

Kerber, Linda K., *Women of the Republic: Intellect and Ideology in Revolutionary America.* University of North Carolina Press, 1980.

Labaree, Benjamin Woods, *The Boston Tea Party.* Oxford University Press, 1964.

Langguth, A. J., *Patriots: The Men Who Started the American Revolution.* Simon & Schuster, 1988.

Levine, Bruce, et al., *Who Built America? Working People & The Nation's Economy, Politics, Culture and Society.* Pantheon Books, 1989.

Maier, Pauline, *American Scripture: Making the Declaration of Independence.* Alfred A. Knopf, 1997.

——, *From Resistance to Revolution: Colonial Radicals and the Development of American Opposition to Britain, 1765-1776.* Alfred A. Knopf, 1972.

McCullough, David, *1776.* Simon & Schuster, 2005.

Morgan, Edmund S. and Helen M., *The Stamp Act Crisis: Prologue to Revolution.* University of North Carolina Press, 1995.

Nash, Gary B., *The Unknown American Revolution: The Unruly Birth of Democracy and the Struggle to Create America.* Viking, 2005.

Norton, Mary Beth, *Liberty's Daughters: The Revolutionary Experience of American Women, 1750-1800.* Little, Brown, 1980.

Quarles, Benjamin, *The Negro in the American Revolution.* University of North Carolina Press, 1961.

Robinson, William H., *Phillis Wheatley and Her Writings.* Garland, 1984.

Wilson, Susan, *Boston Sites and Insights: A Multicultural Guide to Fifty Historic Landmarks In and Around Boston.* Revised edition. Beacon Press, 2003.

Wood, Gordon S., *The Radicalism of the American Revolution.* Alfred A. Knopf, 1991.

Young, Alfred F., *George Robert Twelves Hewes, A Boston Shoemaker and the Memory of the American Revolution.* Beacon Press, 1999.

——, and Terry J. Fife, with Mary E. Janzen, *We the People: Voices and Images of the New Nation.* Temple University Press, 1993.

Zagarri, Rosemarie, *A Woman's Dilemma: Mercy Otis Warren and the American Revolution.* Harlan Davidson, 1995.

Zinn, Howard, *A People's History of the United States.* HarperPerennial, 1995.

Zobel, Hiller B., *The Boston Massacre.* W. W. Norton & Company, Inc., 1970.

Index

Numbers in italics refer to photographs, illustrations, or maps.

☆GPO:2006—320-367/20009 Reprint 2006
Printed on recycled paper

National Park Service

Picture Sources

Most of the photographs and illustrations credited below are restricted against commercial reproduction.

Front cover Boston Athenaeum; 2-3 *Boston harbor* American Antiquarian Society, *teapot* Colonial Williamsburg; 4-5 Carnegie Museum of Art; 8 *Long Wharf* Bostonian Society, *portrait* Thomas Gilcrease Museum, Tulsa; 10 Marquess of Zetland, Richmond, North Yorkshire, England; 12-13 *map* National Park Service; 12 *sugar advertisement* Boston Athenaeum, *map* Boston Public Library, *ship* Peabody Essex Museum, Salem; 14 Museum of Fine Arts, Boston; 16-17 Louis Glanzman; 20 Massachusetts State House, Boston; 22 *printing press* American Antiquarian Society, *newspaper* Bostonian Society; 24 Museum of Fine Arts, Boston; 25 Bostonian Society; 26-27 ©Louis Glanzman; 27 *portrait* Massachusetts Historical Society; 28-29 *effigy print* Library of Congress; 29 *portrait*, National Portrait Gallery, *stamps* Massachusetts Historical Society; 30 *blacklist* New York Public Library, *portrait* Brooklyn Museum of Art; 33 Boston Athenaeum; 34 Christ Church College, Oxford, England; 36-37 ©Louis Glanzman; 38 Massachusetts Historical Society; 40 *troop landing* (detail) Winterthur Museum, *soldier* ©Don Troiani; 41 Boston Athenaeum; 42 John Carter Brown Library; 44 Museum of Fine Arts, Boston; 46-47 ©Louis Glanzman; 48 Museum of Fine Arts, Boston; 49 Bostonian Society; 50 *tea chest* Daughters of the American Revolution, Boston Tea Party Chapter; 50-51 *engraving* Library of Congress; 52 Steve Dunwell; 54 Yale Center for British Art, New Haven; 56 Museum of Fine Arts, Boston; 57 *lantern* Concord Museum, *list of colonial dead* John Carter Brown Library; 58-59 Michael Tropea; 60 Brown University Library; 61, 62 Chicago Historical Society; 63 *portrait* Lexington Historical Society, *powder horn* Chicago Historical Society; 64, 65 Museum of Fine Arts, Boston; 66 Massachusetts Historical Society; 68-69 ©Louis Glanzman; 70 *flag* Massachusetts Historical Society, *slave petition, portrait* Library of Congress; 71 *African Meeting House* Joanne Devereaux, *portrait* Massachusetts Historical Society; 74-75 James Higgins; 77 Steve Dunwell; 78 National Park Service; 81, 82, 83 Steve Dunwell; 85 *Old South Meeting House* Joanne Devereaux, *Old State House, Old Corner Bookstore* Steve Dunwell; 86 Ancient & Honorable Artillery Company, Boston; 87 Steve Dunwell; 89 *Old North Church interior, Copp's Hill Burying Ground* Steve Dunwell, *Revere House* Paul Revere Memorial Association; 91 *Bunker Hill Monument, U.S.S.* Constitution Steve Dunwell, *Charlestown Navy Yard* James Higgins; 92 National Park Service; back cover Steve Dunwell, except *Revere House* Paul Revere Memorial Association, *Old South Meeting House* Joanne Devereaux, *Faneuil Hall* James Higgins.